Arcade Repair: Asteroids

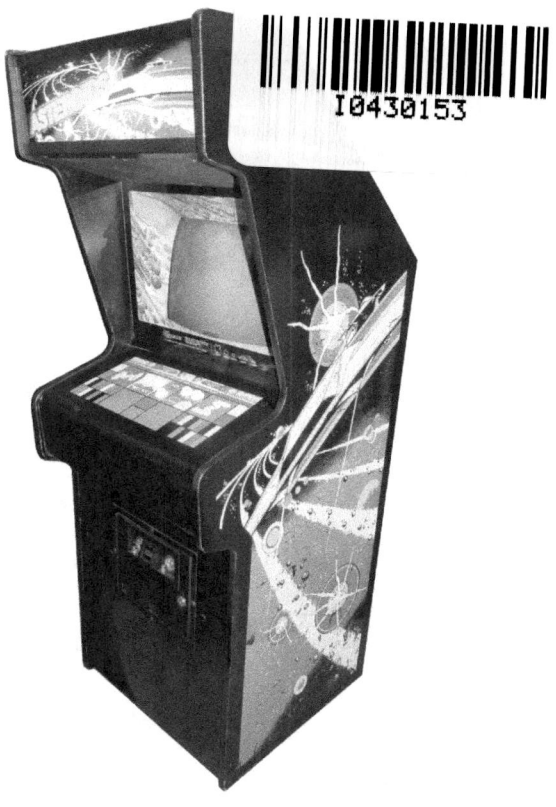

I0430153

A practical repair resource for problems

with a 1979 Asteroids arcade machine.

By Scott Elder

Contents

Introduction   1

General Troubleshooting   4

Cabinet   13

Coin Door   23

Marquee and Lighting   32

Control Panel   41

Power Supply   46

Game Board   54

Monitor   67

Other Information   75

Wiring, Pin-outs & Dipswitches   78

Introduction

Arcade machines are great fun to have at home, be it one machine or a whole roomful. They're fun to play, great to look at; a real snapshot of days gone by. There is a downside however, and not that they are simply heavy. They do break occasionally, preventing them from being much fun. The problem can be anything from a minor button sticking to a more major issue of a monitor going up in smoke.

This book will introduce you to common repair techniques and show you particular repairs and weak points specific to this game. Some take very little mechanical skills while some are quite advanced. You should not attempt repairs you don't feel comfortable doing, and you risk personal injury and the possibility of doing costly and nearly irreparable damage to your game. That said, depending on your location and financial resources, you may have little choice but to repair them yourself. There's nothing wrong with learning something new, right?

Some of the basic tools you'll need may include:

Phillips, regular & torx screwdrivers
Security bits & driver.
Soldering Iron & thin gauge solder
Desoldering vacuum
Multimeter (ohmmeter + voltmeter + diode test)
Wire jumpers
Small needle nose pliers
Fine tip side cutters
Allen wrenches
Various wrenches & sockets for larger assemblies
Original Owners Manual

The owner's manual is particularly well done for Asteroids. This should have a part number of TM-143, and there were many revisions made and published by Atari. Later revisions are more inclusive with fewer mistakes, but there were several revisions made to the games, so if you don't have the manual that shipped with your game, the manual you buy may not match your game parts 100%. It will be close, but particularly around electronic components, there may be differences. This book is not intended to replace the factory manual, as it is full of copyrighted reference material that will not be covered here.

Regarding the soldering iron, you can get away with an inexpensive larger iron if you're doing larger wire repairs on things like buttons or power supplies, but if you intend on doing circuit board work like replacing capacitors or IC's, you really should invest in a mid-grade unit. It should have a fine point tip like a sharpened pencil and be temperature controlled. Most circuit board work can be done around 500 degrees.
It's very important to solder properly. When working on a circuit board, it should only take applying the iron's tip to what you're soldering (or desoldering) for a second or two. If solder isn't flowing quickly something is wrong and you risk burning up components or burning traces off the board. Solder needs a good clean surface to flow to. When desoldering, sometimes you need to add a little new solder to get the old oxidized solder to melt well before using your solder sucker to remove it. Anytime you are not trying to save the old component, try to first clip it off the board before attempting to remove the legs.

Another common practice is to always use a quality IC socket when replacing chips. PC boards will frequently not tolerate being soldered in the same place twice, so desolder and remove the chip, solder in a machined socket or socket strips and be done with it. Sometimes the dead chip you're replacing is just a victim of another problem, so you may end up burning up another one before the real culprit is identified, which is another benefit to using a socket.

Some more advanced tools you may find useful include:

High voltage probe to detect/bleed off CRT anode
Logic Probe
Oscilloscope
CRT Rejuvenator

This book is broken apart by the various major portions of the game. Of course a problem may overlap multiple areas. For instance, if you're seeing no image on the screen, is it a power problem, a game board problem or a monitor problem? That's always the first step in diagnosing, so get started and fix that machine.

This repair guide mostly deals with the common Asteroids version, which is the upright dedicated cabinet. The first few hundred games were released in reclaimed Lunar Lander cabinets and there was also a cocktail table version. Most repairs will apply, but there will be some differences. There is also a factory set of schematics that are very useful. It's marked as drawing package DP-143.

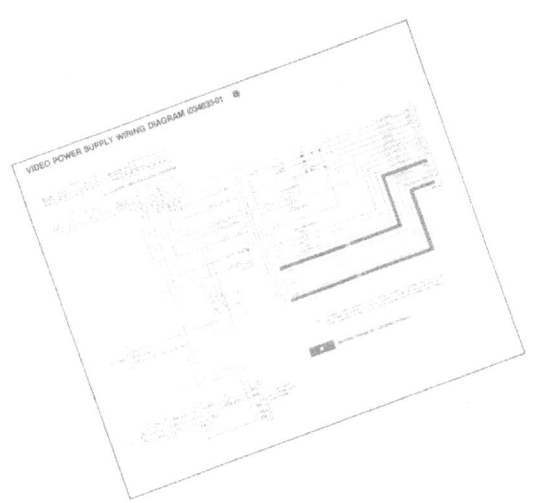

General Troubleshooting

Getting started with your repairs usually falls into two categories. You either have a good idea of where the problem is or you don't. An example of the first is if the game mostly works, but one button isn't working. So you know the area to start (control panel) and know which button isn't working, so you know how to start your debugging. In this case, you would want to start at the control panel and look at the physical button. Of course the problem could be much deeper in the wiring or on the game board, but you know where to start. On the other end of the spectrum is when you have a game with no picture on the screen. It could be wiring, power supply, game board, or monitor all causing the 'dead game' problem.

The following is a general guideline of how to get started.

Be positive the game is plugged in and has power. Sounds obvious, but a faulty plug or power strip can happen.

When you turn the game on, are there any signs of life? If marquee light isn't lit, the coin door lights are dark and you don't hear any kind of startup hum, begin with the power supply section. If you see lights or hear sounds, then you're getting at least some of the power sources to the game that it needs to run. At this point you should try to determine if the game board logic is up and running. Try adding credits either by dropping coins in or manually flicking the credit switches (typically) on the backside of the coin door. If you hear a sound when the switch is activated you have some level of game board activity. After adding credits, press the start button. Do you now hear some game play noise? If so, then your game is 'flying blind', meaning it's likely to be running and the problem is in the monitor.

Some games will have LED's on the game boards or power supply boards, so if you remove the access panel on the back of the game you may see some activity on a seemingly dead game.

When you have access to view the back of the monitor, look near the end of the glass neck on the monitor you should see a faint orange glow. If you see the glow, along with hearing a bit of static build at the monitor as you turn the game on or off, there is a fair chance the monitor is actually working. Be very careful around the monitor as there really is a lethal amount of voltage present.

If you really don't know where to start with a dead game, start at the power supply. It's really the heart of the game and should lead you to the problem.

There are some basic testing procedures that you will use while troubleshooting, mostly are around the use of your multimeter.

A multimeter is a necessary tool when debugging video games or pinball machines.

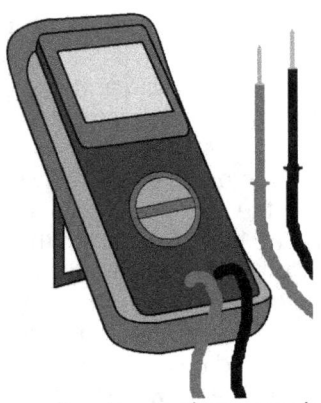

They may be called a voltmeter or ohmmeter but really those are just functions of a good multimeter. You'll want one that checks voltage ac & dc, resistance, preferably one that has a simple continuity check that beeps, and a diode test. The good news is that most recent multimeters sold have all these features. The better brands will be more accurate, last longer and may have more auto-ranging features. If you don't have auto-ranging you just have to start at higher voltage settings to figure out where you need to be set to. Auto-ranging is really nice because you basically just pick the function and you're ready to go.

Here is a simple explanation of the various functions:

Volts DC Symbol

Voltage testing is simply measuring the voltage that's present across two points. When measuring DC (direct current) voltage, you simply put the black meter lead on a ground point (indicated on wiring diagrams as ground, earth, -, negative) and the red lead on the voltage point to check. If the meter auto-ranges, you really don't need to pay attention to red/black lead orientation. If you put the leads on backwards, the voltage will simply read "-5.00v" instead of "5.00v". For typical debugging it won't make much difference. Logic devices, like the game board will typically want right around 5 volts to run stable. Some games will run between 4.90 to 5.25 volts, but most should be around 5.05 volts. Sound boards often use 12 volts, which will sometimes read from 12 to 15 volts.

Volts AC Symbol

Reading ac volts is similar, you don't need to worry about which lead goes where, there is no ground, just two ac points to touch. There are some voltages you should not check, if you know they're extremely high, most meters will not handle it and possibly be ruined. These voltages are ones that are stepped way up like monitor flybacks running around 16,000 volts.

Ohms/Resistance Symbol

Checking resistance is used mostly on video games to check that a connection is made or that it's open (not connected). If you put your meter on resistance, or, better yet it has an audio continuity setting, now touch the ends of the two leads together. The display should show 000 or something very close to that, and if you have audio it will beep. It indicates the leads are either touching (closed circuit) or not touching (open circuit). You always do resistance or continuity testing with the game power off. This is very important, as you can damage your meter and possibly your game if the power is on. You will use this test a lot. If a button isn't working, you can easily test the switch itself by putting your meter leads on both leads of the switch and activating the button. It should indicate closed circuit (000) when the button is pressed. If it doesn't, you start using your meter to check the wiring leading up to the button. Using wire jumpers to extend your meter leads you could check continuity all the way from the switch on the control panel to where the wire enters the game board. Again, always test with the power off.

Diode Symbol

Diode test is used not just on diodes, but on many other electronic components such as chips and transistors. There are some simple techniques for using diode test that will help you find faults without really understanding much electronics. If you have a known good game board and a bad game board, and lots of patience, you could probably find the problem using your diode test. A very common practice is to test similar components and look for differences. This would usually mean finding a similarly numbered component, either on the same board or another board, and measuring their pins with the diode test.

Here are simple examples of how to test some common components. There is one big caveat with this due to ways the board is wired, you may have to desolder and lift one or more legs out of the circuit to get valid readings. Other components wired in place will throw off your readings.

Diodes

These are kind of like one way valves. They let electricity "flow" through them in one direction but not the other. With your meter on diode test, put the red lead on the non-banded end, and your black lead on the banded end.

The meter should read somewhere between .4 to .65. This isn't a hard and fast range, you'll see the occasional reading of .3 or .7 but most will be in that range. If you now reverse your meter leads, it should now read 0. That's because the diode is blocking your meters voltage from flowing that direction. Diodes will frequently be able to be tested while mounted in the circuit, but if you find one that reads out of range, desolder one end and test again.

Transistors

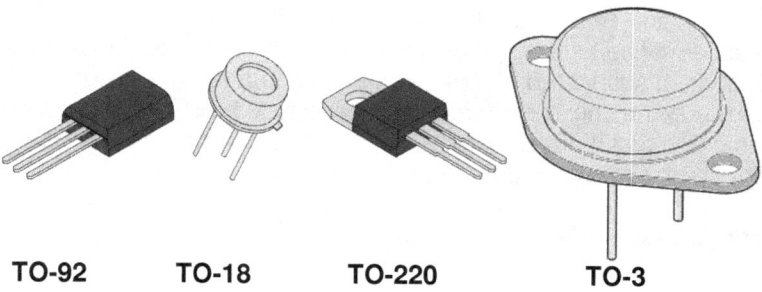

TO-92　　**TO-18**　　**TO-220**　　　**TO-3**

Without knowing the much about type of transistor and how it's supposed to function, you can still do simple diode testing to spot a bad transistor. You basically measure across all combinations of pins and make sure they all either read open (0) or between .4 & .65. For a three leg transistor there are six combinations to read. Some metal cased transistors only have two legs and the metal casing is equivalent to the third leg. Again, frequently you can test in circuit, but when you find one that is testing bad, you need to lift the leg out of circuit and retest. The idea with diode testing is that usually when they fail they tend to go way out of range, and frequently short (read 000).

IC's

Similar to a transistor, you're looking for a combination of pins that are way out of range of "typical". If you're lucky you'll find an identical chip nearby and be able to compare the two. You'll potentially make four passes across all the legs of the chip with your meter on diode test. You need to identify the plus and minus volt pins of the chip. These usually have larger traces nearby and you'll see those large traces run to several other

9

nearby chips. Now you place the red lead on one of the two pins you've identified and take the black lead and start testing all the other pins. They should read from .4 to .65. If they read 000 then you have a suspect. You now put the red lead on the pin your black lead was previously on and test all the pins with your black lead. Repeat the last two steps, only using the 2nd pin that you identified as being one of the plus or minus pins. When you identify a suspected bad pin, you should first try to test another of the same chip, and if the chip happens to be socketed, pull the chip and test it out of circuit. See the section on the game board for steps on how to remove IC's.

Resistors

Placing your meter on resistance testing, you simply place a lead on each end of the resistor. Lead orientation does not matter. This is much easier with an auto-ranging meter. The grey area with resistors is knowing what value they are supposed to be, and then realizing they can be up to 10%-20% off and still be ok. You either have to have schematics showing what the values should be, or, a reference chart or software (phone app) to look up the values. Resistor values are designated by the color of their stripes. Some large resistors, usually the large white sand/ceramic resisters will actually have their values printed on them. Occasionally a resistor will go out of range, but most frequently will short or go open. All in all, they are fairly robust.

Capacitors

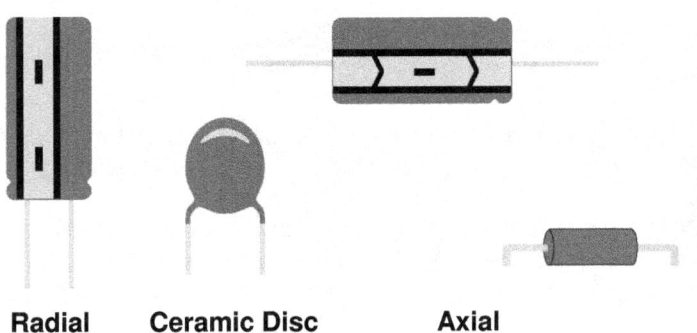

Radial   **Ceramic Disc**   **Axial**

You can't really test capacitors with your multimeter, only look for really bad failures. If you test with your meter on resistance setting, you'll usually see some sort of resistance value, and frequently it will rise the longer you hold it. If you reverse the leads you might see it look like a short (000) and then start rising from there. Other times it will simply look like a short. You may find a bad one by comparing values and behavior to a similar capacitor elsewhere on the board. On aluminum electrolytic capacitors (barrel shaped with aluminum ends), you may see physical signs of problems. They may swell and even burst at one end, or show signs of leakage. There are dedicated tools for checking capacitors but they are fairly spendy units. In some circuits, notably on power supplies, you can measure AC voltage across the two leads of larger capacitors and it should be fairly low. If it reads more than a volt or so, it may be bad.

Fuses

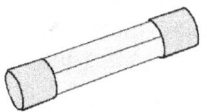

        Fuses are just like testing a piece of wire. Place your meter on resistance or continuity test. Place leads on each end of the fuse and it should read near 000 or beep. You should always pull at least one lead of the fuse out of its socket before testing or the circuit it's attached to may give you a false positive. Regarding fuses, there are several different physical sizes, so pay attention to that when replacing them, but more important than size is the value rating. There are three things that you need to match up when replacing the fuse. The first is if it's a slow blow or fast blow (sometimes called time delay fuses). Fast fuses will blow immediately upon the fuse exceeding its rating, slow fuses have some amount of time before burning. Slow blow are frequently designated with an MDA or MDL marking. It's difficult to simplify the intended use, but a lot of times electronics such as game boards will be protected with a fast blow fuse, items like coils or motors will use a slow blow as an occasional exceeding of rating isn't that unexpected. The second rating is

11

voltage. You should match voltage as close as possible, but there are occasions where your replacement will be slightly higher rated. The third rating is amperage. This is most important. This is the amperage rating at which the fuse will blow, consequently preventing damage or fire in your electronics. It is very important to use the manufacturers suggested values when replacing fuses. Many people, particularly newcomers to game repair will stick in higher rated fuses, so don't simply replace fuses with the same value, look up the correct value in your owner's manual and use that. Whatever you do, don't run a jumper wire or wrap foil around a fuse to make the connection. Fuses blow for a reason, and effectively removing them will likely cause components or wires to overheat and melt, possibly starting a fire. People have stated that 'jumping' the fuse will identify the 'bad' part, but frequently it will ruin an unrelated part, such as a voltage regulator that can't tolerate being grounded out because of another bad part. Occasionally an old fuse may just fail, though it's pretty rare. When a fuse fails, you will normally replace it and see if the new one fails. If it does, you need to start chasing that problem. If the new one does not, you may have experienced a premature fuse failure, or, some other trigger that caused the fuse to fail has not happened again. At the prices of fuses, if you are chasing a problem that keeps blowing fuses, you may want to build yourself a tool like this.

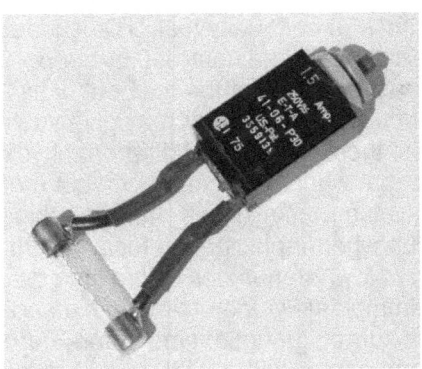

It is a mini-resettable circuit breaker with its leads soldered to the top of an old blown fuse. You can put it in place of a fuse, and you'll hear it pop if it blows. It can simply be reset instead of blowing a buck each time like when using fuses.

Cabinet

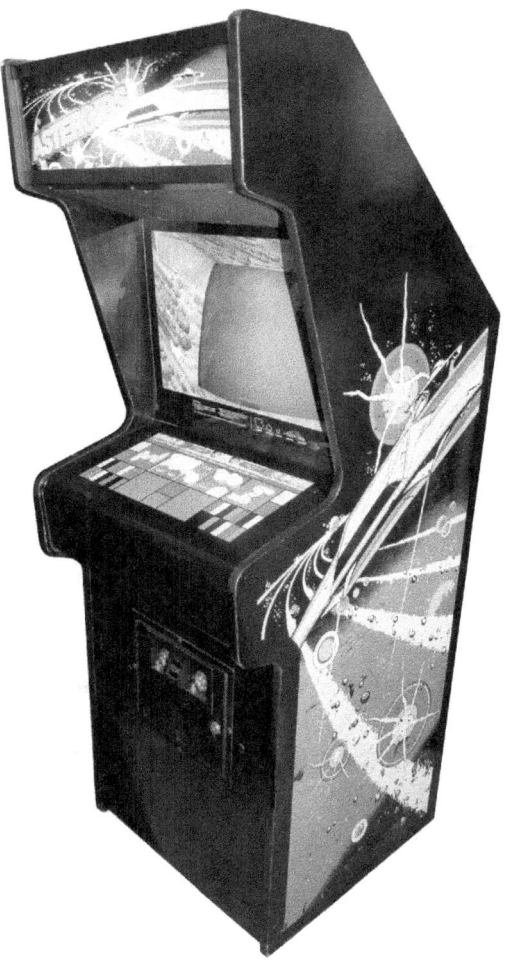

A cabinet has a couple purposes. The first is to be a sturdy enclosure to hold all the delicate internal parts while holding up to the abuse of people hitting and kicking it. Its second function is to provide a place for artwork. Some games take full advantage of this and have artwork and clever design built-in throughout the cabinet, while others may just have art on the side or on the marquee.

If your cabinet has structural issues you need to address these as you would any wooden cabinet repair, using common woodworking techniques. Some of these cabinets have been stored over the years in places that cause a lot of swelling and shrinking of the wood, and some of the glues used may vanish over time, leaving a cabinet that will really be ready to fall apart under its own weight. Sometimes you can re-glue the major panels and clamp them while drying and tighten a cabinet right up. Other times, if a panel really has a lot of damage you may need to replace it, particularly if it's the floor of the game as that provides the feet (usually screw in metal levelers) stability.

Leg Leveler

Whenever you acquire a game, you should look under it for the condition of the leg levelers (or feet). If you've slid it on its back into a pickup to transport, before you unload it is a great time to check them out. You'll frequently find games that are missing feet. Sometimes they're just simply unscrewed out of the t-nut and gone. More often the wood wore around the t-nut and allowed it to fall out taking the leveler with it. Once one foot is gone the game won't stand upright correctly and so sometimes you'll find one that was broke out and the rest removed so the game will sit flat. When the feet are missing there may be sharp edges that can damage your flooring, so if you're considering using a game without feet, make sure there are no staples or metal plates that will touch your floor. Replacing the T-nut is usually not a problem. A good hardware store should carry them, and they may even carry the levelers. On some games it's

14

a steel plate with either threads cut in to receive the foot or a nut welded on for the same purpose. Because the wood at the bottom of a cabinet occasionally will have weather damage, you may find that you need to do some real woodworking to repair/replace part or all of the flooring. The good news is there is usually extra room in the bottom of these cabinets, so if you need to mount a little extra support on the inside of the cabinet it can be done in a way to not affect the outside cosmetics.

Another common issue is for an access panel, usually the main back door, to simply be missing. It's usually just a task of cutting a new panel to the right size and painting it, but don't overlook venting. When replacing panels you should look at the factory design and see if there are details you need to pay attention to. Venting is the primary thing, though occasionally you'll see a panel that has special cutouts to allow room for something like the neck board on the back end of the monitor. The hole for mounting the ¾" locks on these panels are typically an inch away from edge, usually centered across the width. Asteroids back door is 23 3/4" by 36 3/16" with the lock centered in the width.

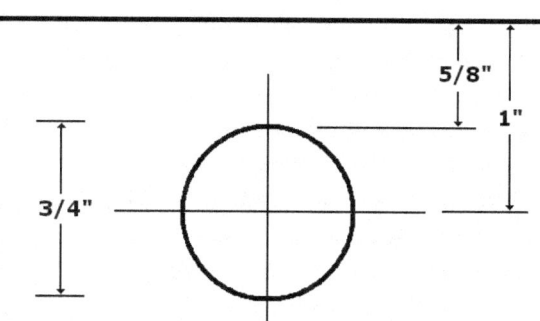

Typical Lock Drilling Location

Cosmetic blemishes are the most common problems with arcade cabinets. Here are some typical issues.

P: Holes drilled through wood, frequently happens near coin door to bolt on additional security bars.

A: Slightly bevel the edge of the holes with rough sandpaper or a larger drill, fill with Bondo (two-part filler, same as used in car repair). When it is just starting to set up, use a razor blade to level it to the surface. After curing, lightly sand it smooth, touch up with matching color paint.

Cutaway shows original hole damage on left, right shows it after being prepped for filling.

P: Large crack running through wood, usually on a narrow spot near control panel or monitor. Likely a result of damage from the cabinet actually tipping over while being moved.

A: First step is to make the repair structurally strong. This may mean gluing and screwing a plywood panel on the inside of cabinet if there is room. You'll also want to inject wood glue as deep as possible into the crack. Depending on the extent of the crack, sometimes you can get away with just paint touch up after gluing, sometimes you'll need to use body filler. If you use filler, you should probably cut or sand the edges of the crack to remove loose raised pieces and give the filler more room to feather along the edge.

Cutaway shows original crack damage on left,
right shows it after being prepped for filling.

P: Entire corner of side is broken off and missing. This is usually
from moving the game and catching the very corner on
something (hand truck).

A: If this is a very small piece missing, say under an inch, you
can clean up the damage with a razor knife and rough
sandpaper and rebuild the corner with body filler. Larger pieces
usually involve cutting the old wood off cleanly and fitting a
replacement piece of new wood. Ideally it would be doweled and
glued on all edges where it meets other wood, reinforced with
plywood on the inside and then prepped with body filler on the
joined edges much like repairing a crack. The good news here is
that it's usually a bottom corner where there is no artwork, so if
you prep it well, you can usually make it blend by simply using
spray paint of the appropriate color. Rustoleum makes an
excellent grey primer that builds up fairly well giving you a nice
surface to fine sand before painting. It's found in most stores
near the automotive body repair products.

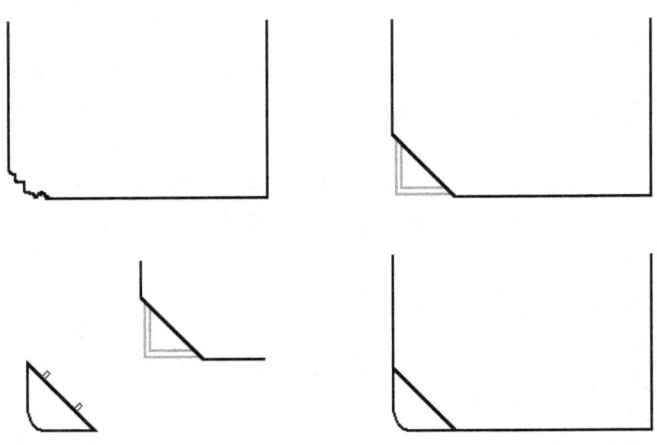

Corner damage, cut it out cleanly, build a new
piece, glue and re-inforce in place and paint.

P: There are large scratches through the painted on artwork.
This may include scratched in graffiti or initials.

A: You can do a remarkably nice job touching up scratches with
the common acrylic paints sold in most craft stores. They are
very reasonably priced and come in hundreds of colors. If you
can't purchase just the right color, they mix very well to match
just about any color you need. There are a couple tricks. You
need to match the color after they dry. They tend to dry a little
darker than they look wet. They are also typically flat, not
glossy. You can spray gloss over them, or brush on clear acrylic
gloss paint to match a glossy finish cabinet. They will fill fairly
large scratches, as the paint is sold thick, but can also be
thinned a little, brushed into scratches and then you wipe off the
excess leaving just a little paint filling in the scratch.

P: The wood grain or very minor scratches are showing through the paint and holding dirt stains. The cabinet doesn't clean up like it should.

A: Very carefully use a product called 'Magic Eraser'. It's a foam pad that will get into the surface and lift dirt. You can use it with water or rubbing alcohol (it will wear out fast using alcohol, but it cleans really well). Use it with caution as it can dull paint or cut right through it, particularly if the paint is well oxidized. You may need to polish cabinet afterwards.

P: The overall finish on the cabinet seems to be dull or faded.

A: Like polishing any surface, similar rules here apply. You can buff it using a paint polish, but you run the risk of pushing the wax or polish deep into scratches or wood grain, so you typically only want to do that on very smooth finish cabinets. Wax will make paint not stick, so If you plan on touching up afterwards use a wax-less polish, like Meguiars #7 or Novus #2. Sometimes a faded cabinet simply cannot be 'buffed' back to life. In some rare circumstances you could lightly scuff the cabinet with a fine scotchbrite pad and actually repaint it with clear automotive paint to gloss it back up.

P: Metal trim parts, like around the marquee are faded, scratched or rusted.

A: Obviously a repaint is in order. Here are the proper steps. Remove the part from the cabinet and fix any imperfections like dents first. Usually a small hammer and a block of wood and you can tap things back to their factory shape. Now strip the old paint off. Spray or brush on paint stripper may be used but it's messy and sometimes ineffective. Normally a wire wheel on a bench grinder will strip the paint and rust right off. Immediately clean it with something like Naptha or enamel reducer and once it's dry, spray on a good coat of primer. As recommended earlier, Rustoleum auto body primer works well. It's important to primer it quickly as rust will form on the freshly stripped metal very quickly. Once the primer dries scuff it down with some medium sandpaper like 180 - 300 grit. You may want to prime it again. Now use finer, 400-600 and give it a quick scuff. Now using appropriate color and finish, probably black, and finish, frequently satin, spray several light coats until its color and finish is perfect. You really can put on very professional looking finishes with cans of spray paint, it's mostly in the prep work.

P: The plastic t-molding on the edge of the cabinet is ratty, torn, or missing. How do you replace it?

A: Most of the parts houses sell it, as do some dedicated websites and you can find the common stuff on ebay. It's a fairly simple process. Tear off all the old stuff, be a little gentle because over the years someone may have glued it down and being too aggressive could splinter wood and damage the finish. On some cabinets it's stapled at the ends to hold them down. The staples are sometimes painted over as part of the finish, so remove the molding gently if it seems to be mechanically attached. You may want to leave the staples intact and just notch the new t-molding to fit around them. Clean up the cabinet edges once the t-molding is removed. Now would be an excellent time to do any paint touch-ups on the cabinet edges. T-molding comes in a few basic colors, sizes and styles. Most classic arcade games used ¾" either smooth or textured. Start re-installing the new molding by cutting a nice straight cut in it and start tapping it into place at wherever the original started at the front of the cabinet. A rubber mallet is the proper tool. You may want to cut small "V" shaped reliefs into the back of the molding for two reasons. If there are staples or nails still in the cabinet that you need to work around and when you are tapping it around corners. Usually around the corners of the control panel, if you just snip two or three little V shapes out, it will fit the contours very easily. Not required, but it goes into place easily. If you find it's not staying tightly in place everywhere, a hot glue gun will fix it right up. Apply the glue to the wood, directly in center of slot and then quickly tap the molding down into place. It seems to be common practice to use hot glue under the ends to keep them secure, which is probably better than nailing and risk splitting the wood.

P: The paint is worn or chipped on the monitor bezel.

A: Clean the back with mild soap and water and touch up the area using either hobby grade acrylic paint or touch-up paint markers. Since the paint is on the back and light doesn't shine through, it's very easy to make very good repairs on the bezel.

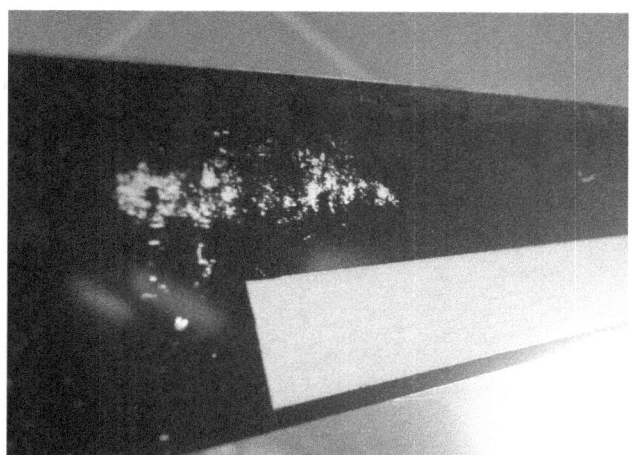

P: The clear part of the plexiglass monitor bezel isn't very shiny or has small scratches.

A: Clean the plexi well with soap and water on both sides. Try polishing with a polish like Novus #1. You simply spray it on and buff it back off with a soft cloth. You can buff the unpainted portions of the plexi using a product called Novus #2 plastic polish or an equivalent. If that is not removing the scratches you can first try buffing with Novus #3 (it's a much more aggressive compound). Big scratches, like someone scratching in initials or graffiti can sometimes be removed or at least partially cleaned up by sanding out the scratch with a super fine grit wet/dry sandpaper. Use 600 to 1200 grit, using water to keep it wet, and then polished when done. There is a bit of an art to polishing plastic and you may not be successful your first few tries, so be warned. You should always avoid any kind of harsh chemicals on plexiglass/lexan. Cleaners like carb cleaner, electrical spray, goof-off, brake cleaner etc can melt and ruin the plastic. Unlike a marquee, most monitor bezels that have artwork on them are not backlit, so you can do much simpler touch-ups. All you need to generally worry about is matching the color.

Coin Door

Coin doors really take a lot of abuse in the lifetime of an arcade game. The outside is hit and kicked and scratched, not to mention simply being touched by hundreds or thousands of grimy hands. The inside of the coin door is most susceptible to damage once the game has been adopted by a private owner, and the lock either left open or removed. Once that happens you have people blindly sticking their hands in the mechanisms trying to find the elusive coin switch so they can add a few credits. If you're lucky the damage will just be some bent coin switch wires, but it can mean broken wires or missing parts.

Asteroids upright cabinets came with one of two different styles of coin doors. The earlier machines had the flat round coin slots shown below.

Here is the more conventional door found on most machines.

Mechanical issues with the coin door are usually fairly obvious. These might include broken coin mechanisms, broken/sticking coin return buttons or linkage, coin return flaps, those type of problems. Other problems will be things like the coin switches or lamps not working. We'll address the common ones with our standard (P)roblem / (A)nswer format.

P: Coin door is locked and you don't have the key.

A: You need to break in. Here's the standard ways to do that. Try to get in through the back door. If it's also locked with no key, it may be best to drill out the back door lock rather than the front. Any damage you may do to the cabinet would be best in the back. Usually you can drill right through the center of the lock with a 1/4 " drill bit until the cam on the back of the lock falls off, allowing the door to open right up. Sometimes one of the back panels will be held on with screws that can be removed allow access to the lock without drilling. If it's a "new to you" game, make sure the key isn't stuck in the coin return slot or screwed onto the back of the cabinet or zip tied along the power cord. It's often possible to use a screwdriver to pry open the door, but it always damages something, usually either bending metal on the door or breaking out a piece of wood. There are some ultra strong lock cams out there that will refuse to bend. You'll occasionally run across a lock that will be tough to drill so you may be need to try the prying approach, if you do, be sure to protect prying surfaces with wood or cardboard as much as possible.

P: Coin switches are not racking up credits.

A: Put the game into test mode, mounted just inside coin door.

Do you hear any buttons working as you press them? If playfield buttons work, but coin ones do not, check the plug in where all the wires from the coin door run into to. Look for broken wires or pins. Next, with the game off and the coin door wiring harness plug undone (unplug it to remove any connection between the switches and the game board). Now check for continuity between the two wired pins on one of the switches using an multimeter. The switch should read open (0) with switch at rest, and when switch is clicked it should read fully on (000), just like you put the two leads of the multimeter together. If switch isn't working properly it will need replaced. Occasionally you can bend one of the leads on the back and it will begin making contact but that is typically a short lived fix. Also ensure you can hear the switch click. If it's not clicking it may be a horribly bent coin trip wire. If the switches test good but still not working in test mode, you'll need to test the wiring continuity all the way from the switches to the game board. This will prove if it's mechanical (wiring/switch) or a problem on the game board.

P: The coin door is ugly, scratched, paint is chipped off and worn off from use.

A: Coin doors are painted using several types of paints and textures. It is very difficult to match original textures, so whenever possible, if the damage is slight, you should consider just touching up the areas. If you use the correct style of paint (flat, matte/satin or gloss), you can repair chips very well. If the door is in need of a complete repaint there are a couple options. If it's in fairly clean condition but just needs a fresh coat of paint, just scuff the existing surface with a fine scotchbrite pad and spray a thin layer of paint over it. That preserves the stock texture. If you need to match textures you'll have to experiment with some of the available products, but there are generally two styles, one that creates a fine even texture, somewhat like a fine sandpaper, and others that creates a very large/uneven pattern. Either way, if you can't get them in exactly the correct color or style, you should be able to spray over them with another paint to take advantage of the texture. If the texture paint is flat, you may want to cover it with some clear or gloss black to give it a longer life and make it easier to clean.

P: Lamps that should light up the coin entry slots are not working.

A: First check the bulbs. You may find building a tool like below to be very handy to test bulbs.

26

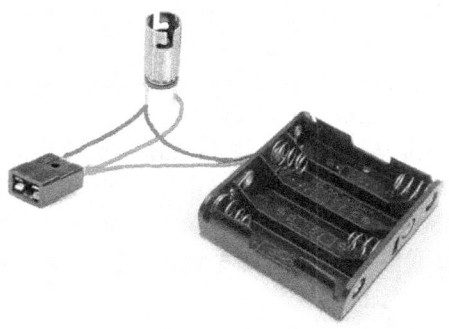

So either test them or replace them, making sure they are the correct style. Asteroids typically used #47 bulbs. If they are still not working, check for around 6 volts with your multimeter across the two lamp wires. If the correct voltage is not present you will need to backtrack the wiring all the way to the power supply. Examine the plug on the coin door wiring for broken pins or broken wires.

P: It won't accept coins.

A: Stock the machine would only accept quarters. There are adjustments on the removable coin mechanisms to adjust for slightly different sizes of coins, but if you are trying to run tokens you should use ones that are very similar sized to a U.S. quarter. Check that the coin chute and coin accepter mechanism are lined up with each other and are mounted properly. If the coins are jamming, not rolling through, attempt to determine where they are stopping at. Typically it's either in the top chute, inside the coin mech, or at the bottom as they drop through the slot at the coin switch. The coin mech can easily be removed and you can drop a coin through it to test. A bent wire on the coin switch can also stick when a coin hits it.

P: It accepts coins with the door open but when I close the door it no longer accepts coins.

A: There can be a few reasons for this. Sometimes the lid on the coin box is misaligned, not letting the coin fall all the way into the box. This is usually fairly easy to identify, as when you open the door you see or hear the coin fall through. Another problem can be the coin accepter coil, see details below. The most obscure reason is perhaps the machine is not very level. Coin flow through the door counts on the machine being reasonably level to allow the coin to roll through everything correctly.

P: Coin falls straight into coin return slot.

A: Usually this means the coin is being rejected by the coin mechanism. There are a few reasons. Sometimes the "Reject" button was pressed, which spreads open the coin mech and lets coins fall out and drop into the coin return slot. If the coin mech sticks open any new coins will reject. It can happen because you're not using the right sized coin for the coin mech, or the coin mech is improperly adjusted. Another common problem is that there is a powered circuit on the coin door that activates a coil when the machine is powered on that trips a lever on each coin mech that allows them to take coins. The idea behind it is that if the machine is powered off, any coins will simply reject and be returned.

It's not uncommon for this coil to be defective or tampered with, and not properly allowing the coin mechs to accept coins. On home use machines there is a trend to disable the coil, as it draws a fair amount of power and runs warm when the machine is on for hours. The way this would normally be done is something like remove one of the wires from the coil and tape or place shrink tubing over the wire so it can't touch anything, then use a small zip tie to fasten the plate near the face of the coil to simulate the coil being activated.

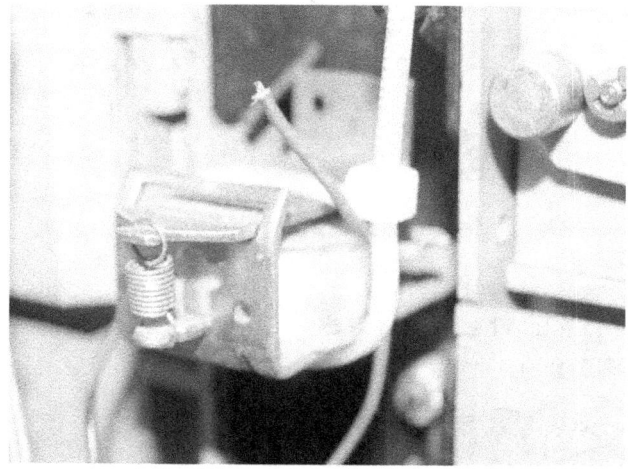

This just replaces the coil needing to hold the trip switch on and allows it to always be on.

P: Coin door has holes drilled in it, don't like it.

A: This is a common issue. A previous operator probably bolted on a lockdown bar that when across either the lock on the door or across the whole door. It was a safety measure to keep coins locked up safely. The doors are usually just mild steel so it's possible to have the holes welded over, ground, puttied, primed & painted, it's just not very practical. Most doors were com used on several games so they're not too hard to turn up used. The most common fix though is to just locate some carriage bolts that are just big enough the head covers the hole and using a nut just attach it through the hole. You may want to paint the head of the carriage bolt black before installing.

Carriage bolt covering hole in coin door

If for some reason it's a really large hole, they make bolts with very large round heads called Elevator bolts. They can cover large damaged areas.

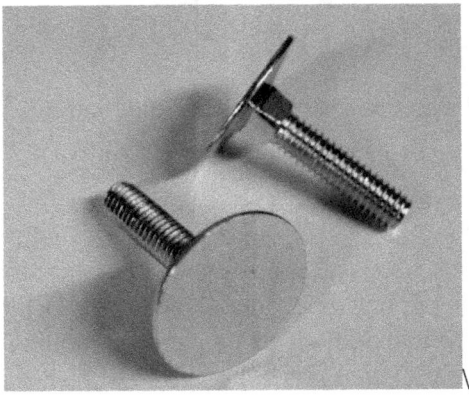

Large head elevator bolts

This door had a large pushbutton mounted in it, an elevator bolt painted black will cover the hole and make it far less noticeable.

Of course, some times you'll see damage like below, where a lock was sloppily installed. You'll need to fix the cabinet wood damage, but the coin door will likely need replaced if you're doing any kind of restoration.

Marquee & Lighting

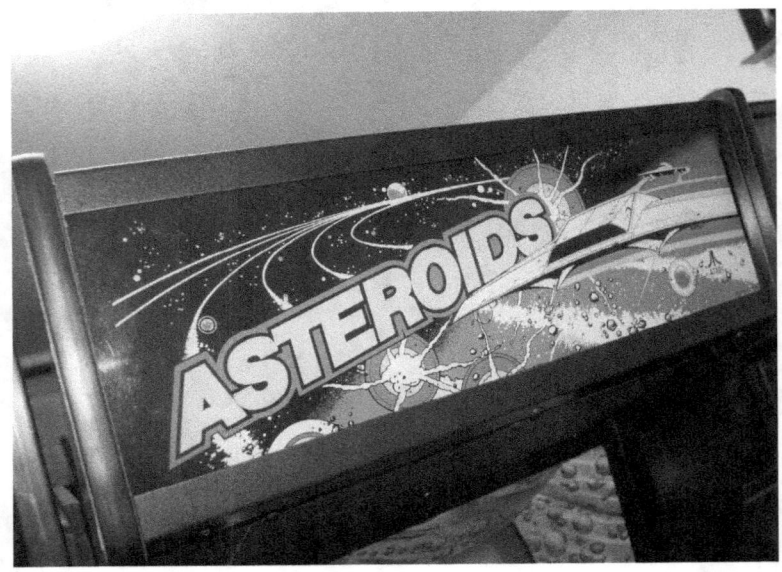

The backlit marquee is probably the first thing you see on a game as you enter the room. It's a focal point of the art package of the game. The marquee itself is very simple, it will either be glass or plexiglass with artwork screened on the back.

You remove it from the game by taking out the screws holding the top metal trim.

These were originally Allen head machine screws with a star lock washer. There are only a few things to do with the actual marquee itself. If it's broken or very badly scratched up, you'll need to replace it with a used one or a new reproduction. Typically the reproductions are simply mylar sheets (thin plastic) that need affixed onto a piece of clear glass or plexiglass with a little tape. Used marquees should be plentiful at online parts houses or ebay.

It may just need to be really well cleaned. If it's glass, the front can just be cleaned with any good glass cleaner, like 409.

The back however needs to be treated very gently. If the paint is still 100% attached you should be able to clean it with a barely damp soft cloth, but don't rub hard. Use of any liquids increases the risk of wiping paint off.

Plastic marquees can be polished on the front. Clean them well with soap and water. Best success will be had with a small car polisher like this one.

Low speed buffer

You can buff the front using a low speed buffer with a terry cloth pad and a product called Novus #2 plastic polish. If that is not removing the scratches you can first try buffing with Novus #3, it's a much more aggressive compound. Big scratches, like someone scratching in initials or graffiti can sometimes be removed, or at least made much less visible by sanding out the scratch with a very fine grit wet/dry sandpaper. Use 600 to 1200 grit, wet with water, and then polished when done. The painted side of plastic marquees tends to be a little tougher than when on glass. You should be able to clean it with the same soap and water used on the front. You should always avoid any kind of harsh chemicals on plexiglass/lexan. Cleaners like carb cleaner, electrical spray, goof-off, brake cleaner etc can melt & ruin the plastic. When working on the front of the marquee, you'll want to set the painted side down on a large soft cloth or foam pad to avoid damaging the paint.

The last polishing technique we won't cover here, but you can research if you're motivated is called 'flame polishing'. You can use a propane torch to polish plexiglass, but it takes practice and the surface needs to be prepped and cleaned well. It is very easy to destroy the surface rather than fix it.

Another marquee problem is if it contains scratches or chips in the painted side. The truth is it is almost impossible to perfectly touch up a lighted portion of the painted image. That said, you can make small repairs that will make them far less noticeable. If you're lucky, it's in a masked or 'blacked out' area of the paint, where it's intentionally blocking light. Those areas you simply fill them in, typically using acrylic craft paints. To finish the repair, you can paint over the touched up area with a little silver or white to match the factory finish. Those hobby paints are available everywhere for very little money and come in a lot of colors.

Acrylic hobby paints

To touch up areas where light is supposed to show through is much trickier. It counts on the paint being very even and partially translucent. The acrylic hobby paints do not work very well for that, with the exception of the specialty ones that are designed to 'slightly' mimic stained glass. You may have better luck with enamel paints, thinned with clear paint to make them even more translucent. Touching up lighted areas is really a skill that must be learned through trial and error. Just remember to keep paint even, wipe off any excess or thick areas, and try your color matching in the least intrusive area first, knowing the color may change as it dries. There are a couple other tricks, one being the use of an airbrush to spray the paint evenly and thin, and in conjunction with that, instead of touching up part of a given color, you scratch away all of the color in a damaged area and re-spray it all, avoiding the need to perfectly color match. For example, there's a 1" x ½" blue stripe that has a big flake knocked out of it. Rather than have to match the exact blue, using an exacto knife, scrape away the whole 1" x ½" area and re-spray the whole area. A lot of work, but it should end up looking good.

Light fixtures in these games can be very problematic at times, which is a little silly considering how simple they really are.

There are just 5 parts that can cause problems, listed here in order of likelihood.

1. Starter

When power is first applied, the starter will heat the filament of the bulb to 'jumpstart' it. If the starter is not working the bulb will never light. The simplest way to diagnose the starter is to simply swap in a new one. If you start to remove it (twist counter-clockwise) and then put it back (twist clockwise) and the bulb lights, then the starter is bad. Pay attention to rating when buying a new one. There are common sizes of FS-2 (14W, 15W or 20W up to 24" bulbs), FS-4 (30W, 40W 36" or longer bulbs) and FSU (universal). Asteroids uses an FS-2 starter.

2. Bulb

Fluorescent bulbs will fail in various ways. They will start dimming or turning pink from losing mercury, the ends will heat leaving dark burns on the inside. The lamp may start flickering. If the lamp displays any of these symptoms it needs replaced. If it will not light, you may need to replace it. The simplest way to verify is to swap in a known good one. You should probably keep a matching spare in the bottom of the cabinet anyway, so do a quick swap to check it. Sometimes they will look brand new, but a broken filament is preventing it from heating and starting.

Asteroids uses an F15T8. Original equipment was the large diameter glass, but most of them for sale now are thinner, around an inch in diameter.

3. Wiring/Connector

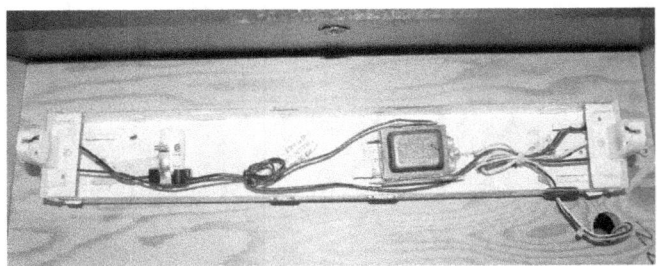

You shouldn't have much problem with the wiring, but you need to check voltages and test connectors. Usually there will be a two or three pin connector up near the fluorescent lamp fixture. There are also wire nuts making connections that can come loose. Carefully check input voltages by testing for AC 120 volts somewhere near where the bigger wires enter the fixture.

Here's a generic lamp wiring diagram to refer to if you suspect the wiring in your game is wrong.

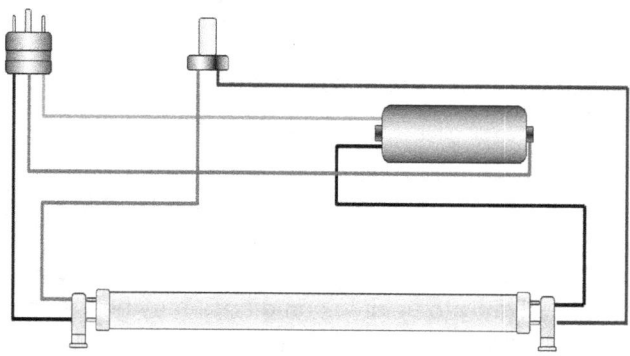

4. Ballast

Basically if you have tried a new starter and bulb, have verified voltage and still don't have light, it's time to suspect the ballast. Any store that has a good lighting section should sell them and the tiny ones these games use are usually very inexpensive. Another symptom of a bad ballast is if you replaced the bulb and it came on very bright for just a second then went out, a bad ballast may have just destroyed the filament in your bulb.

5. Bulb mounts

These mounts seem really flimsy and breakage prone, but the rarely fail in a way that wiggling the bulb won't cause it to light. If you frequently have to turn the bulb slightly to get it to come on, it may be the fault of these sockets (although that is sometimes your hands grounding the bulb, indicating you may need earth ground fixed to the lamp frame). Also inspect where the wires enter, as they are usually just cheap press-in terminals. Sometimes you can take apart the socket, bend terminals slightly to increase gripping force and re-insert wires. Always be careful of the high voltage around these when power is applied.

Control Panel

Asteroids has a fairly simple control panel. There are five buttons with leaf switches underneath them and two lighted start buttons. The graphics are painted on and textured. Though fairly durable, once they wear it's difficult to touch up a very large area. Fortunately there are several companies that made replacement overlays. They look great, the downside is being a more conventional overlay they don't feel quite the same. To gain access to the control panel, open the coin door and at each side underneath the control panel there should be a wing nut that you can remove. Pay attention to washers underneath the nut, as they will want to fall down into the game. Originally there was a large flat washer and a lock washer above each wing nut. Over the years they may have vanished, or more often than not, they're lying in the bottom of the cabinet.

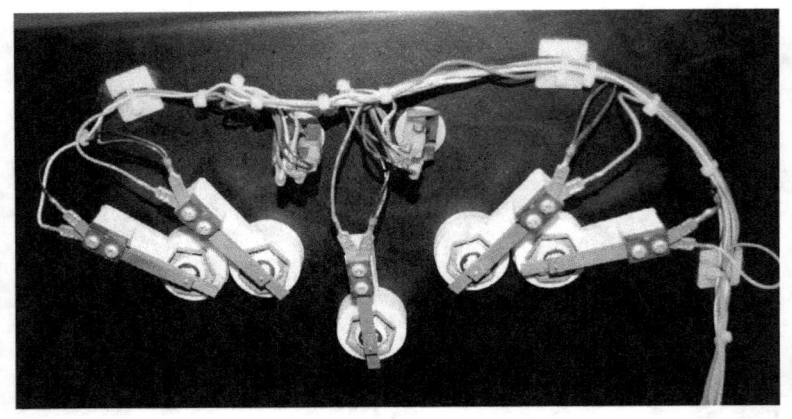

Looking at the panel from the inside, you can see how the buttons are mounted. They should be gold plated switch blade contacts, meaning you should not file or sand them, to clean them simply put a piece of paper or card stock between the points, use a finger to push the top blade down a bit to put pressure on your paper, and pull the paper through the contacts to clean them. It's not recommended to use any cleaner or electrical contact spray. As far as adjustment, that's a little bit of a preference thing. Technically they just need to make contact about halfway through the button stroke, but on Asteroids in particular, some people will set them up very tight, leaving a gap about the size of a business card. Set up tight you can almost just 'wiggle' the button to make it go. It is important to the feel of the game to have all buttons adjusted equally, if you barely have to touch 'left', but have to push 'right' all the way in to make it go it may distract from the game play.

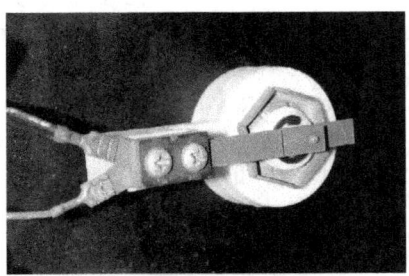

You adjust switch blades by making sure they are both as straight as possible, then you make slight bends in the outer blade. There is a specialty switch blade adjustment tool available from pinball parts suppliers very inexpensively, but for a few switches you can just use small needle nose pliers. A properly adjusted switch makes a slight wiping motion at the contacts as they make contact. This wiping helps self-clean the contacts. You may find that someone has replaced the entire button assemblies with the more common micro-switch style. They don't use a pair of blades, they just have a small switch attached at their base. While these work well in a lot of games, they do not work very well in Asteroids. There are some ultra smooth and fast reacting switch style buttons that will be acceptable, but for the most part none are fast enough to give you the same play as the blade switches. The clicking alone will disrupt game play, but you will also notice you can't keep your bullets gapped tightly.

Generally nothing much goes wrong with these control panels besides needing the occasional switch cleaning or adjustment. The small zip tie holders may come loose allowing wires to hang and flex, so you may find a wire detached from the switch, but it should be very rare. The entire switch circuit, including the wiring and game board is fairly robust on Asteroids, so you shouldn't encounter many problems.

P: A button isn't working or intermittently works.

A: Clean switch, ensure gap is correct (approx. 1/32") and that wires are firmly attached.

P: No buttons are working

A: Make sure game appears to be running correctly and you can add a credit to it (look on screen for credits). Do the start buttons flash? If so, does the game start? If nothing on the control panel is working check the main connector that attaches the control panel to the main wiring harness. There is also a common ground wire between all the switches, you may need to locate and test that it is attached and making contact all the way from the game board to the control panel. If the game starts and none of the game controls work you have a fairly odd scenario. Again, check the common wire between all the switches. You may have a game board problem.

P: One button is much stiffer or softer to press.

A: There are a few things that can make a button feel different. First compare the switch blades under the odd button, looking to see if they have been replaced with something not comparable to the other switches that feel correct. Buttons tend to pack up with dirt and soda and whatever else works its way in there. You can remove the plastic button assembly by removing the large nut. That assembly can normally be taken apart and inspected and cleaned by removing the metal C clip. Not all aftermarket buttons can be taken apart without damaging them. Once apart you can clean them using soapy water and a toothbrush. While apart you will see obvious problems like if they're bent or cracked and rubbing, or if the small spring is broken. Different brands of buttons use different spring tensions, and occasionally the springs will simply break. This can cause an unbalanced feel between buttons. Of course the buttons are readily available and fairly inexpensive so you may want to simply replace them all with a matching set. Be aware though that some brands are not as high quality as the stock ones.

P: How do I remove the start buttons from the control panel?

A: The top cones screw on, with one hand on cone, other on the switch, twist switch a little to loosen cone and then unscrew.

P: There's a cone missing on a start button and the button fell into the control panel.

A: There are now aftermarket cones available. Before that they were becoming very hard to find. They usually have a thin sheet metal nut on them that is an adjustment for the height (and they are a fairly common thread size for panel switches if you need to find a nut) so as a temporary solution you may be able to just use a nut above the panel.

P: One of my start button lights isn't flashing when credits added.

A: The switch contains a small lamp that while possible to replace is not very practical. You first need to identify if the lamp is burnt out or if power is not getting to it. Add at least two credits so both lamps should be flashing. Assuming one is flashing, the easiest test is to simply swap the lamp leads from the base of the working switch to the base of the non-working one.

P: Button is not working, switch tests ok, wiring and connectors test good.

A: Test/Replace L13 IC

Power Supply

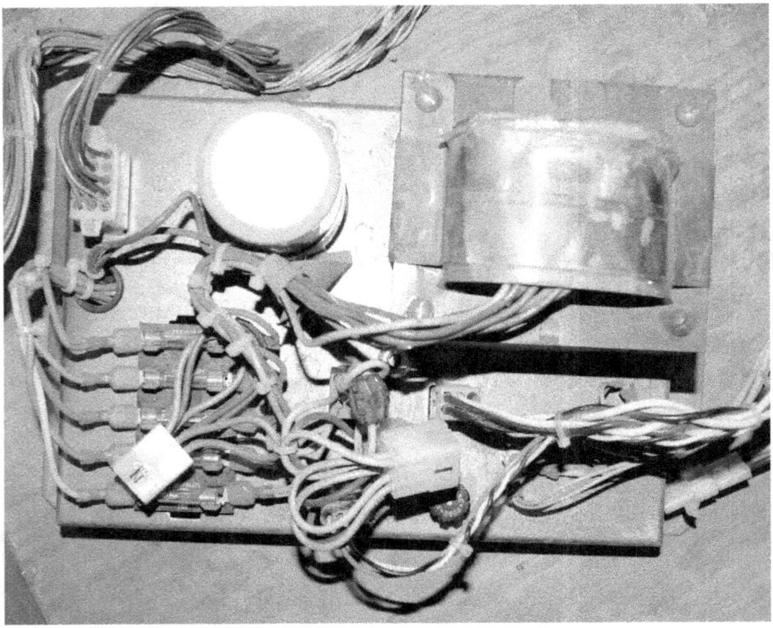

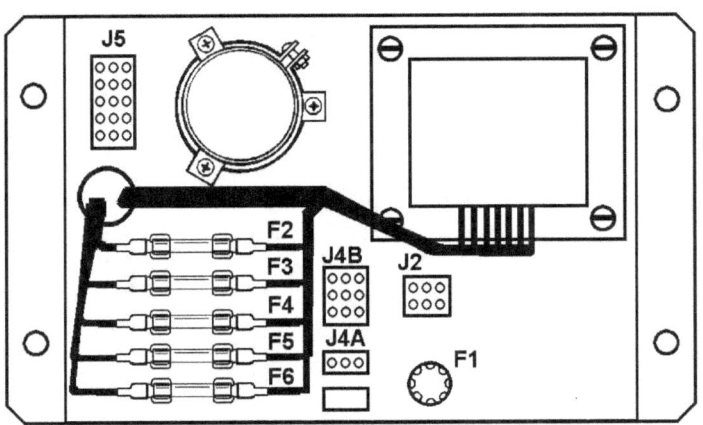

Top View

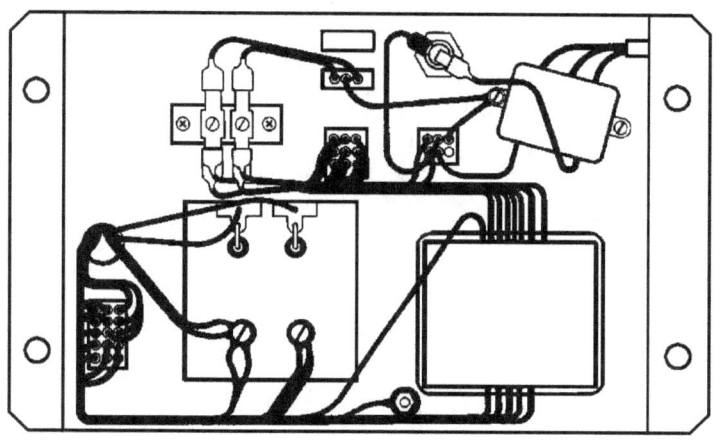

Bottom View

The power circuit really starts at your wall plugin or power strip where you're plugging in the game. Assuming we're talking a US model game, it expects to plug into a conventional 3 prong outlet providing around 115 volts ac. You can test for that with your multimeter by measuring across the two rectangle plugin holes with your meter set on AC volts, probably 200Volt setting if it doesn't auto-range. Be sure to always set meter settings properly before inserting test leads. The third round pin on your plugin is the earth ground. With these games it's very important that they be grounded. The earth ground wire runs to various metal parts of the cabinet. If the original 3 prong plug has been replaced with a 2 prong, or, the ground wire cut or broken off, you really should replace it before powering on the game. The ground wire can prevent shocks and absorb static electricity that can damage components and even cause things like the fluorescent bulbs to not start properly.

This raw ac power is typically fed into the game directly to an RFI filter. While it's possible for this to be faulty internally, it's very rare. You can easily test for 115 volts AC at both ends, it should simply pass it through.

One lead of the AC goes through the fuse located on the power supply assembly. Unplug the game and pull the fuse (push down and twist it counter clockwise), and then test it using your meter on continuity or resistance setting. You should get 000 reading.

The AC power is now fed through the main power switch and safety interlock switches, if they are still intact. Over the years if an operator suspected a failure they may have wired around the switches. AC power is ran through these switches in series, so any one of them that's open will cut the AC volts. The power switch is on the bottom left of the cabinet when you're facing it from the back. There is an interlock switch that detects the back

48

door is closed and another interlock behind the coin door to verify it's closed. A properly functioning interlock can usually be pulled out to turn the power on, although some are just push to power on switches. These switches can all be tested with the power off using your meter on resistance or continuity setting. They should read 0 when off, 000 when activated.

If a game is completely dark, showing no signs of life, take a good look at this preliminary power wiring. If the main power supply is not getting its 110 volts, it'll act like it's not plugged in.

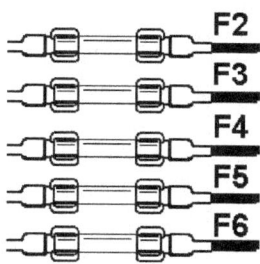

With the power off, test fuses F2 through F6. If you find a blown one, be sure to replace with the correct size.

F1, F2 & F3 = 3 Amp 250V 3AG Slow Blow

F4, F5 & F6 = 7 Amp 250V 3AG Slow Blow

The Atari wiring harnesses are built really well, so unless it's been poorly repaired (hacked up) or exposed to extremely harsh conditions causing connectors to corrode or mice have chewed things up, it should be very dependable and you'll likely never see any issues where the wiring itself is bad.

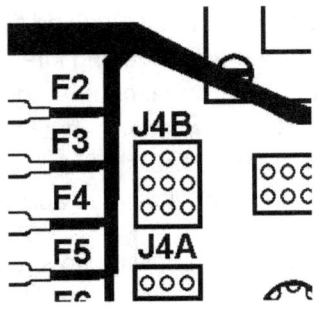

The power supply does have a voltage selection jumper plug (J4B, sometimes referred to as J3 depending on the schematic). Information provided by the manual states the following:

90 – 110 Volts AC uses VIOLET plug

105 – 135 Volts AC uses Yellow plug (standard)

200 – 240 Volts AC uses Blue plug

220 – 260 Volts AC uses Brown plug

The Yellow plug should be used in the US, and in case you need to build one yourself, it's jumpered like this.

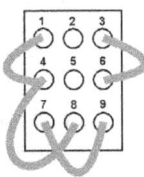

Pin 1 to pin 4 to pin 8, Pin 3 to pin 6, Pin 7 to pin 9

If you suspect the voltage is not jumpered correctly, or there's been some wiring changes made, remove connector J5 and test for proper voltages. Disconnecting J5 will keep the out of range voltages from going to game boards and monitor. Without a load, voltages may read a little higher than specified.

J5 Main Power Output

1 – 10.3V DC (Orange)
2 – 10.3V DC (Orange)
3 – 10.3V DC (Orange)
4 – Ground (Violet)
5 – Ground (Violet)
6 – 36V AC (Red)
7 – 36V AC (Red)
8 – 6.3V AC (Yellow)
9 – 6.3V AC (Yellow)
10 – Isolated AC (Black)
11 – 65V AC (Brown)
12 – X-Y Return (Gray)
13 – 65V AC (Brown/White)
14 – Isolated AC (Black)
15 - Ground

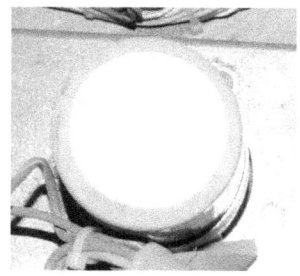

The main power capacitor, commonly called "Big Blue", is a 26,000 uf 15 volt electrolytic. It has a reputation for failing and causing all sorts of game problems. The normal problems with a capacitor failing is they don't buffer the system power very well, causing voltage variances which may make the game to reset or crash. They also pass more AC voltage when bad, causing other issues, frequently causing humming, but it's really allowing 'dirty' DC voltage, so you can have a variety of symptoms. An argument can be made that due to the age of these games, all electrolytic capacitors are past their life expectancy and should be replaced.

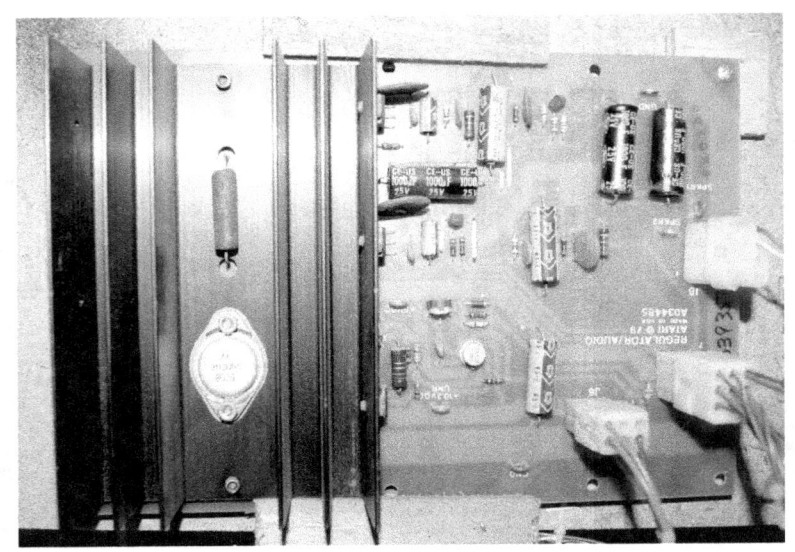

Regulator/Audio Board

The regulator audio board is another critical piece of the power supply. Among other things it produces the +5 volts used by the main game board and is the audio amplifier.

There is a voltage adjustment pot (R8) near the center of the regulator board. This adjusts the main +5 volts for the game board. To test or adjust, locate the +5 test point and the GND test point on the game board. Put your multimeter on DC volts, red lead on +5 and black on the ground test point. With the game on and functioning, check the voltage. Ideally it is very close to 5.00 volts. An acceptable range is 4.90 to 5.20 volts. It should never be higher than 5.50 volts. If it is, clean the game board finger connectors and measure again. If it still is too high, test the +5 volts on the regulator board to determine if it's the regulator board or the wiring between the regulator board and the game board. If you can't bring the voltage up to 5 volts, you likely have a transistor problem on the regulator board, or you have a failed component on you game board that is putting a huge load on the +5 volts. You may be able to 'feel' a problem like this by placing your finger on the various game board chips and feeling for one that's much hotter than the rest.

Problems on the regulator board usually end up either being a failed 2n3055 regulator, lm305 or tip32.

If you aren't hearing audio, the amplifier circuits use a TDA2002AV, driven by a 2n3904 transistor. Audio problems are more frequently a problem with the volume control, wiring or speaker, than a problem with the amplifiers.

P: Testing +5 volts on the audio/regulator board and its showing less than five volts or 0.

A: Test/replace Q3 2N3055 transistor. If good, test/replace Q1 LM305 regulator. Test and adjust voltage after replacing.

P: Loud humming sound is heard over speakers.

A: First suspect the large 26,000 power capacitor. If it's original it may be bad. This will also affect overall game stability. If that doesn't do it look at any electrolytic caps on the game board. Also look at the volume adjustment pot.

Game Board

Atari game boards were made pretty well by the time they released Asteroids. One weak point is the IC sockets . Ram failures are getting more common, as well as game roms failing (frequently oxidized pins) and capacitors drying up and failing. Occasionally you'll see connector problems with the main edge connector, but it's much less often than with a lot of other Atari games, such as pole position. Some boards have problems with the factory soldering. You may find pins or 'thru-board' holes that should be filled with solder but are not. You may need to reflow them with your soldering iron and a bit of solder, though in some cases you may need to run a small wire through the hole and solder to it in order to get solder to flow through hold to each side.

If slightly wiggling the edge connector does things like crash the game, cause resets or make sounds, you may want to clean up the traces on the board using very fine sandpaper (1000 grit) and replace suspect pins in the connector itself.

If you are suspecting a board problem, you should have already confirmed the power supply and auxiliary boards are functioning properly. You should also confirm that you don't have an obvious monitor problem. Is there a faint glow on the crt neck? Is the spot killer lit on the deflection board (covered in the monitor section)? You may be seeing no indications of game logic running, or, you may be seeing objects but they are drawn wrong, or lines are there that shouldn't be.

If you are seeing any signs of life, you should definitely go through the self -test. It's initiated by flipping the test switch just inside the door.

On a properly working game, you should see this screen.

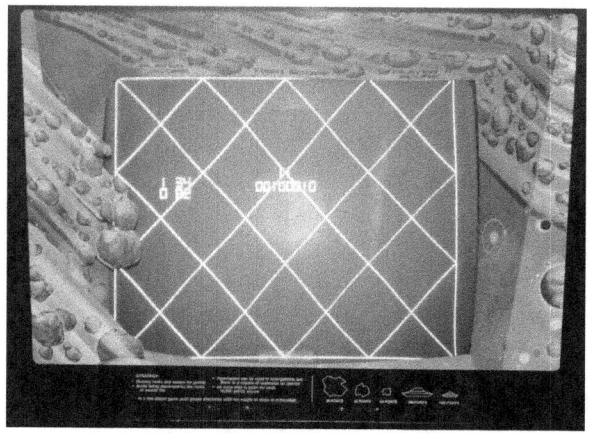

If you get the above screen, the game board cpu is working, at least some of the game code in the eproms is working, and ram chips tested ok. You should also hear a short medium beep indicating it started ok. Player 1 & 2 start buttons should be lit, and pressing any other buttons should cause a high pitch audible beep. In the center of the screen should be a display showing you the current positions of the option dip switch settings.

When working, you can use this display to adjust the monitor. You should adjust size to where the graphics barely fit the monitor, and the lines are all nice and straight. See the 'monitor' section for more details.

When the self test fails, the first thing it has done is test the ram on the game board. If your audio is working, and you have a bad ram chip, you'll hear a series of sounds for each ram that passes, followed by a lower pitch sound indicating failure. For instance, if you hear two beeps followed by a lower tone, it's would indicate the 3rd ram in the chart below is faulty.

1 Tone = Bad ram at location D2
2 Tones = Bad ram at location E2
3 Tones = Bad ram at location M4
4 Tones = Bad ram at location R4
5 Tones = Bad ram at location N4
6 Tones = Bad ram at location P4

If you want to rerun the test, either turn the self test button off and back on, or press the reset button located on the game board.

Reset Button

If you put the game in test mode and the game board appears to not be running, you have a few things to check. As mentioned earlier, always verify voltages on the board. Using your multimeter, test across the ground (gnd) and +5 test points. If voltage isn't correct, work on power supply and/or connectors.

If the board is showing no signs of life, there are a few things you can try. It's not uncommon for the main CPU chip to fail. They are socketed so you can swap in a known good one. If the game seems to be in a pattern of consistently beeping every second or two, usually accompanied by start buttons flashing, that is an indication of the boards 'watchdog' circuit kicking in. The watchdog is monitoring that the board is running, and if it sees a problem it triggers a reset of the board, just like you manually triggering the reset button.

This quickly gets into fairly low level board repairs. If that doesn't bother you, keep reading. If it does, you're probably at the point of shopping for a replacement board or for someone to repair it for you.

It's very important to understand how bad boards can hurt the monitor. If the board is not putting out a good picture signal (telling the monitor how to draw the images), the monitor crt beam sits and burns a dot in the center of the picture tube. They generally have a 'spot killer' safety circuit to prevent it, but it's always a good idea to unplug the power connector up near the monitor if you're going to be powering up the cabinet for more than a few seconds at a time.

If the board is showing no signs of life and you're determined to keep troubleshooting, you can check voltages on the cpu board. There are four voltage regulators on the main cpu board.

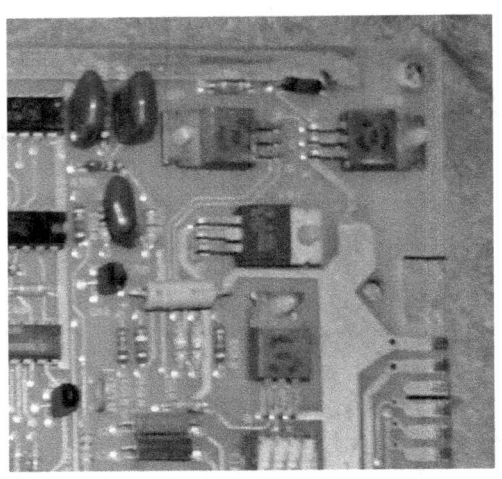

In the above image it shows the upper right corner of the cpu board. The top two are actually transistors, the bottom one is an LM340 regulator (VR1). It has an input of around 22 volts (upper leg) and outputs around 12 1/4 volts (bottom leg).

These three voltage regulators from left to right is a 7915 (VR2) where center leg should be around -22 volts, the output on the right leg should be around -15 volts. The middle regulator is a 7805 (VR3), left leg should be around 22 volts, right leg 5.25 volts. The last one on the right is a 7815 (VR4), left leg around 22 volts, right around 15 volts. Using your multimeter on DC volts and your black lead on ground, carefully testing the legs should provide the voltages stated above.

The game board is broken into a couple of logical sections, the CPU/Sound and the Vector section. The vector section (or frequently called "Vector State Machine" or vsm for short, is located at the lower right side of the board.

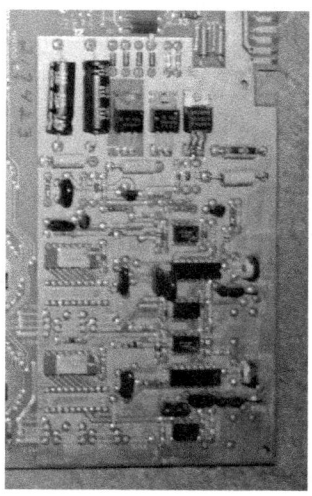

Vector Section

The watchdog circuit can be resetting the board because either section is failing. You can isolate the two by disconnecting pin 1 of the 74LS42 chip at location L6.

IC pins are always numbered like in the above example. They have some indicator, usually a notch, divot or line that indicates the orientation of the IC. Pin 1 is always the first pin counter-clockwise from the indicator. They number counter-clockwise around the chip. You use this orientation marker for placing the chip correctly on the board. The board will usually be marked by a notch or by an indication of which pin is pin 1.

So to isolate the VSM from the CPU section, you need to break the connection of pin 1 at L6. This can be done by desoldering the pin and gently lifting it out of circuit, or removing the whole chip and installing a socket, and when re-inserting the chip you leave pin 1 bent off to the side, or, you clip the pin and later repair it with solder and perhaps a jumper wire.

Once you've lifted pin 1 out of circuit, reinstall the board and try powering it up again in test mode. If you get a short beep and pressing control panel buttons cause a beep, your cpu section of the board is probably running test mode ok (blind because vector section of board is unhooked). This indicates you should focus attention on the vector section of the board, which is generally simpler than a dead CPU section.

There are a few ic's in the vector section that tend to fail on asteroids. The TLO82 amplifiers, usually at locations C12 & A12 are always suspect, along with the TLO81's. The 4016 at B12 & D12 also fail occasionally. Like any IC replacement, you should remove the old IC and replace it with a good quality socket or machine pin strip so that new chips can easily be set in place.

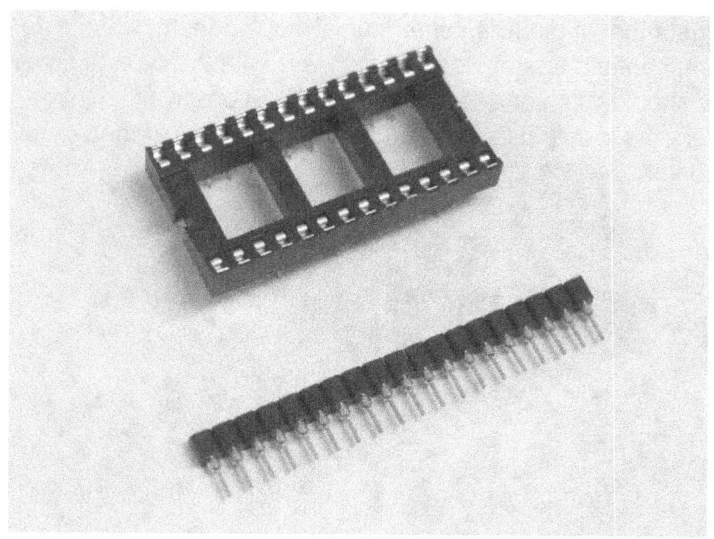

The vector section is made up of a fairly limited number of parts, so using your diode tester you can look for components that are way out of spec and fix the section fairly easily.

If the CPU section is not running, the repairs are sometimes much trickier. While it's certainly possible to locate faulty components, even just using your multimeter, it starts getting very time consuming and complicated. You'll need to have a good copy of the board schematics and understand some basic 74xx logic.

At this point most of you will need to find a replacement board or send your board off for professional repair. If you are a little more intent on finding the problem, there are a few simple things to try, but they start taking resources.

A very common approach is the 'shotgunning' method, where you start swapping all the socketed chips with known good chips. This requires you having extra chips, or more likely another working game board that you can swap from. Start with the CPU, swapping in one chip at a time. There isn't a practical way to test most of the IC's, other than swapping them, without some advanced and spendy tools. As always with this type of scheme, you should swap one at a time so you can positively identify where the problem is, and, you won't lose track of where an IC belongs.

The game roms, or eproms, do occasionally go bad. These can be replaced with programmed 2732 eproms. You can buy an eprom programmer for well under a hundred dollars that will read and write these IC's. You will also need an ultraviolet eprom eraser. There are a lot of choices out there for hobby level programmers, most require a pc with a USB or printer port to plug into. Make sure it will program old eproms such as 2716 & 2732 before purchasing. Some don't do that old of chips.

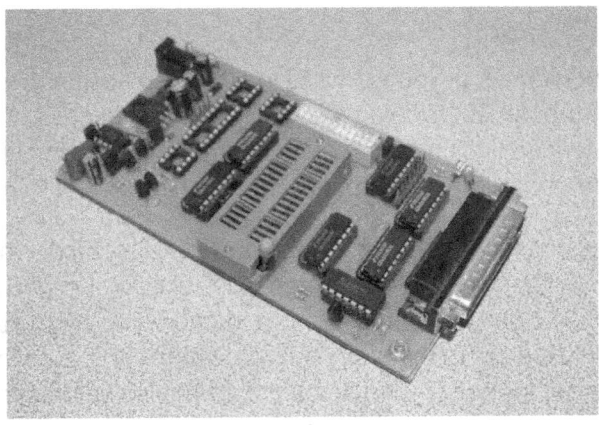

Once you have an eprom programmer, testing the game roms becomes fairly easy. There are a few ways to test. Most programmers come with software that will let you read the rom contents and produce a checksum of the code. Short story is that checksum can be compared to the 'expected' checksum of a proper chip and if they match it's probably ok. Another approach is to download a good copy of the game roms (they are readily available online), then using the eprom programmer you can read your chip and save the results to a file and use a software tool to compare the two files and see if they match. The third approach is the simplest.

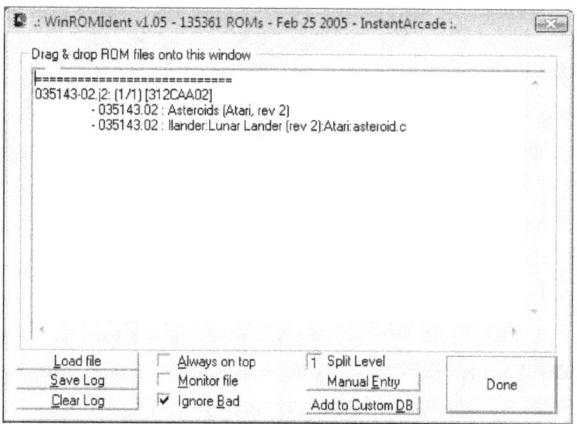

Locate a windows software tool online that is named ROMIDENT (stands for rom identifier). Now find an associated tool named WIN ROM IDENTIFY, it's a user friendly windows front-end for ROMIDENT. You can simply read your rom chip using your eprom programmer, save the contents to a file, and drag and drop that file into WIN ROM IDENTIFY and it will tell you if it recognizes the contents or not. If you buy an eprom programmer, you'll find this utility to be very helpful. It will identify what version of the code it is and usually the socket position of where the chip belongs. It knows the signature of most versions of classic arcade games and pinball machines. Of course if you locate a bad (unidentifiable) chip, you can create a new one using a blank 2732 or 27g32 eprom. Be prepared for the fact that a lot of these eproms are so old now that they may not erase or program properly, so you may go through a few making a good one.

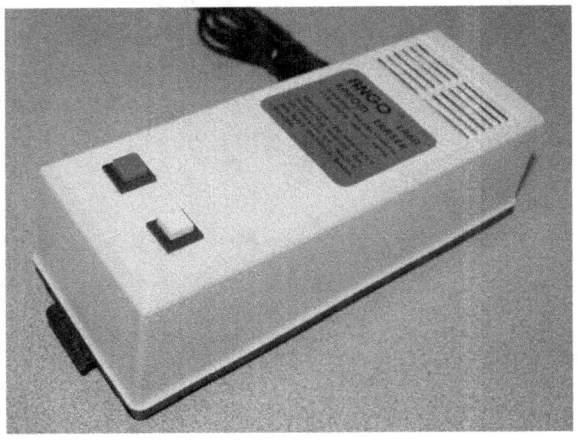

You can erase eproms and re-use them using a special ultraviolet lamp based eraser.

A note about IC locations: While it is a valid approach to swap two identical IC's, proper location of game roms is critical. For instance, if the self-test is identifying a bad RAM chip, the suspect chip could be swapped with another RAM chip and see if the self-test now reports the problem at the new location. That helps you positively identify that the ram is bad. Same thing applies to most other IC's, like those in the VECTOR section of the board. However, even though game roms (eproms) may carry identical part numbers, like 2732, they are custom programmed and are not swappable and must be placed in their correct location. If you're doing work on a game that you've never seen run, there's no guarantee someone hasn't scrambled the position of the eproms. Unlikely, but it happens.

Here are a handful of common repair logs:

P: During self-test, it's showing a ram error. Replaced ram, replaced sockets. It will still intermittently display ram error.

A: if the chip has gold plated legs and the socket is tin, or vice-versa you'll occasionally see weird problems. You'll need to swap one of the parts.

P: Everything seems to work fine, but game play is approximately twice as fast as it should be.

A: There were a few board mods from back in the day when operators were trying to make the game more difficult. You'll need to remove the mods. Look at IC's for a cut leg or perhaps a leg left out of a socket, particularly at C5 pin 4.

P: Explosions appear as lines instead of dot pattern.

A: On boards with REV 04 or earlier, check C9, D9 or E9 74LS191 ic's if seeing horizontal lines, later boards check C10, D10 or E10. If vertical lines, REV 04 or earlier, check F9, H9 or J9, later boards check F10, H10 or J10.

P: Can't adjust width or height of screen, or when I do it jumps past the size I need.

A: It's not uncommon for the adjustment pots to have cracked or have broken leg. Test pot with multimeter (power off), replace.

P: Some characters not drawing correctly or have lines drawn that shouldn't be there.

A: Make sure program eproms are fast enough (300ns or faster). Try swapping in a new set to troubleshoot. May also be the AD651 DAC ic's in the vector generator section of the board. Also check the 7805 +5 volt voltage regulator.

P: When the saucer ships fire, sound isn't correct, just has a tone or a buzz.

A: Test/replace 14016B ic near M9.

P: No ship thrust sound.

A: Test/replace 14016B ic near R12 or LM323 at P11.

P: Background heartbeat thump sound isn't working, either distorted or quiet.

A: Look at .22uf mylar capacitor near C33. If not working or broken legs it can cause sound issue.

P: Some sounds are distorted or quiet, or a high pitch tone.

A: Test/replace electrolytic capacitors on main board, particularly the group around upper left corner of board (C118, C119).

P: What is the difference between a revision B game board and a revision C board?

A: According to an Atari bulletin from Feb 1980, Due to availability problems, prom 74LS399 at A10, B10, C10, D10, E10, F10 were changed to 74LS157 at A10, C10, E10, B/C10, D/E10, F/H10 and 74LS374 at B10, D10 and 74LS174 at F10.

Monitor

Asteroids uses a special monitor, called either "Vector" or "X-Y" monitor. A standard CRT based monitor would be called a "Raster" monitor. The main difference is the approach to drawing on the picture. A raster monitor rapidly draws every line starting at the top left until it reaches the bottom. It then repeats and does this approximately 60 times a second. A vector monitor just points the crt gun and draws just what it wants to draw. It doesn't waste time redrawing the whole screen, it just points and draws the shape. Because of that it's restricted on how much it can draw without flickering, but it draws in very smooth lines.

They haven't produced this style of monitor since the early 80's so parts supplies are dwindling. There are some parts, like the glass CRT that you simply can't order new, so you're forced to either find a good used one or if you're extremely lucky, you might find someone with a NOS (new old stock) one sitting on a shelf. Luckily the CRT (picture tube) was used in a lot of different games, across multiple manufacturers, so it's not too hard yet to track down a used one. They should be interchangeable between any similar sized black & white Atari vector game and between Cinematronics vector games like Star Castle, Armor Attack etc. The other electronics on the monitor are very different between manufacturers, so don't expect to simply swap whole monitors between Atari & Cinematronics.

There is a test fixture called a "CRT Rejuvinator" that will test picture tubes.

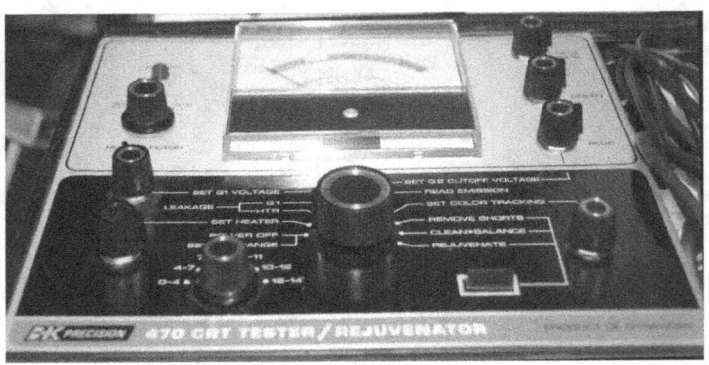

CRT Rejuvenator

It can test the crt for leakage, shorts and even clean the guns, often restoring the picture quality. If your monitor works, but even with the brightness turned way up it still is dim and hard to see, or, the brightness has to be up so high that it's showing lines drawing between screen objects, you may have a bad crt. A rejuvenator is a bit of an extravagance if you only have one or two games, but if you have a row of machines they come in very handy. New they were several hundred dollars, now that crt's are being phased out and tv repairman are retiring, you can pick up a rejuvenator at a fraction of its original price.

Most of them use adapter sockets to fit a variety of crt configurations, so if you buy a rejuvenator, make sure it either has the adapters you need or you can find information on how to build them. A brand name like BK has easily available documentation, even though the tool may be thirty years old. There are times when a rejuvenator will make an unusable monitor picture look like new. Be warned though that during rejuvenation, it's possible the crt gun can be ruined, effectively ruining the crt. It happens very rarely however.

The monitor is made up of various subsystems, we'll present them as follows. The power circuit, the deflection circuit and the high voltage circuit. The power circuit supplies the needed base voltages to the other circuits. It has 5 volt logic power and 100+ volts via the isolation transformer in the bottom of the cabinet. The Deflection circuit is what takes the low power signal produced by the game board when it wants to draw something and it steps up the power to the crt neck coil to actually steer the monitor gun around to do the drawing. The high voltage provides the stepped up voltage via the flyback that the crt requires. Monitor repair could be a book of it's own, we'll touch on some diagnostics and repair that anyone with basic soldering abilities could tackle. It is very important to be careful around monitors, even powered down after several days there can be high voltage that can hurt or kill you, particularly around the large anode that runs up to the CRT.

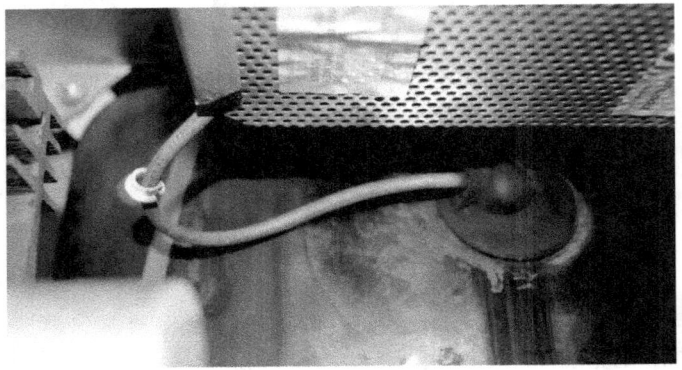

High Voltage Anode

You will probably want to track down the monitor manual for your particular monitor. The most common monitors were electrohome G05's, which had two standard versions. The earliest G05-801 looks like this-

And the later G05-802 looks like this-

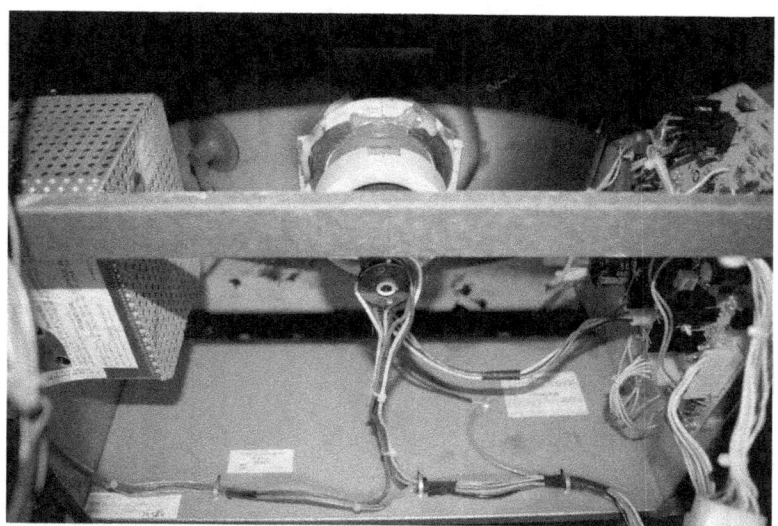

There is a 3rd version from Wells Gardner that you may find, it's a 19V2000. There are enough differences between them that you really need a manual with parts listings and wiring diagrams if you are going to attempt to do any repairs.

The deflection circuit has some fairly common failures we'll cover now. If you see anything on the screen, and the game seems to playing (meaning you can credit up and start a game, as you play it makes thrust and fire sounds etc) it may be the deflection portion of the monitor. This is particularly true if the picture on part of the screen looks fine. The deflection circuit has transistors that power moving the crt gun, and there is a separate transistor for moving up, down, left & right. When a transistor fails it can no longer move the gun in that direction (usually fails completely, can sometimes fail to move it fully). This typically results in a picture where only one half of the screen is displaying, and a collapsed line being drawn in the center.

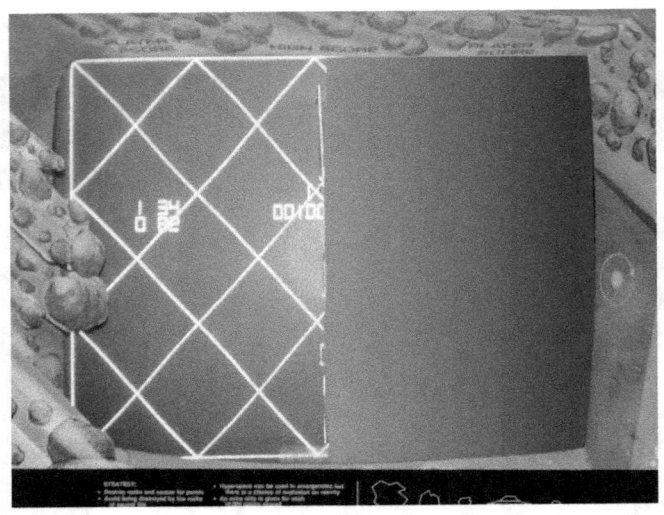

It's possible that problems on the game board can cause similar patterns, but typically if at least one quarter of the screen draws correctly, then the problem is in the deflection portion of the monitor. Fortunately with a diode test function on a multimeter, the main culprit transistors are easy to test. There are smaller pre-driver transistors and large power transistors mounted on the monitor chassis. It's very common practice to simply replace all the transistors at once, and it's recommended to replace the large transistors mounted on the chassis in pairs if not all four at once. If you look at how those large transistors are wired you'll see each pair wire into same harness. You can swap connectors and see if problem changes, if it changes sides then your problem probably is in the large transistors. Be warned that sometimes shorted transistors will take out the smaller ones on the chassis board, so swapping around a bad one might damage others. Normally you would take new parts and swap them in one at a time looking for the bad part. Pay close attention to what you're doing swapping these parts however, there are two different part numbers and you don't want to mix them up.

It's also very common on these monitors to have bad solder joints. Pull the chassis board out of the monitor and reflow the solder on all the connector pins. Bad connections can exhibit the same symptoms as a non-working transistor.

P: You just see faint glowing spots on monitor, they seem to move with the game play.

A: Test/replace TIS98 transistor at Q602 on the monitor deflection board.

P: Brightness fades up and down.

A: It's possibly a bad connection to the heater element on the CRT. You can watch the orange glow at the end of the neck on the back of the picture tube. If the glow fades up and down along with the game elements, it's probably a power issue or bad connectors at the monitor.

P: You are wanting to purchase a used replacement monitor, what games have compatible screens?

A: You should be able to swap in a monitor from other Atari games such as battlezone, lunar lander, red baron and asteroids deluxe. Bally omega race should also work. They are not the same as found in older black & white games such as stunt cycle or space invaders, those are conventional raster monitors. There are color x-y monitors that are found in games such as star wars and although they may be made to work, it isn't very practical to use them because of their cost and they generally aren't as reliable as the B&W.

P: You've repaired monitor or are using a known good monitor and the game elements are not drawing properly.

A: Several similar display problems can be from a faulty deflection circuit in the monitor, or, from a problem in the vector section of the CPU board. If you're satisfied your monitor is working, it's time to troubleshoot the source of the graphics.

P: Brightness is turned all the way up and you can barely see the graphic lines. They all seem to be rendering fine, just dim.

A: May simply be a worn out picture tube (CRT). It may be able to be rejuvenated with success, or you may have to track down a good used one.

Other Information

Here are some bits of information that just didn't fit under any other topics.

Rom Changes & hacks

The M.A.M.E. (multiple arcade machine emulator) which has become an archival reference to game roms list three variations of the roms, versions 1, 2 & 4.

Rom set 1 has two glitches, one is it allows you to hide the player ship behind score display and avoid collisions and if you're thrusting full speed either left or down and turn the ship in the opposite direction it will not slow down.

Rom set 2 has a text change at bottom the says "1979 Atari" instead of the previous text of "Asteroids by Atari".

Rom set 4 allows small saucer fire earlier and fixes a bug where the last initial of the 10th best player gets erased. Atari sent out an update offer to operators that contained an upgraded program rom that would allow the small ship to immediately fire upon the player when entering the screen. The original code waited for ship to travel one-sixth of the screen before firing first shot. There were two kits, if your original rom number ended in -01 you ordered upgrade kit 08-0303009 which included a new AVG rom, if -02 it was kit 08-0303008.

There seem to be very few hacked versions of asteroids roms available. For a game like Pac-Man, you can download hundreds of variations where people have changed the maze or the game characters. There are a few versions out there that do things like give you more lives at the start, but we've only seen one that changed game play.

There is one you may find call Star Destroyer, it changed all the asteroids to star shapes and had different text throughout.

Running on an oscilloscope

You can easily view an asteroids vector output on a two channel oscilloscope. Put it on X-Y mode, ground both leads, clip first lead to 'x output' test point found in vector section of main game board. Place other lead on 'y output' and scale range to fit screen.

Image showing scope leads on
bottom right corner of cpu board

If you happen to have access to a scope, this is a nice way to
immediately tell if a rendering problem is on the game board or
actually the monitor itself.

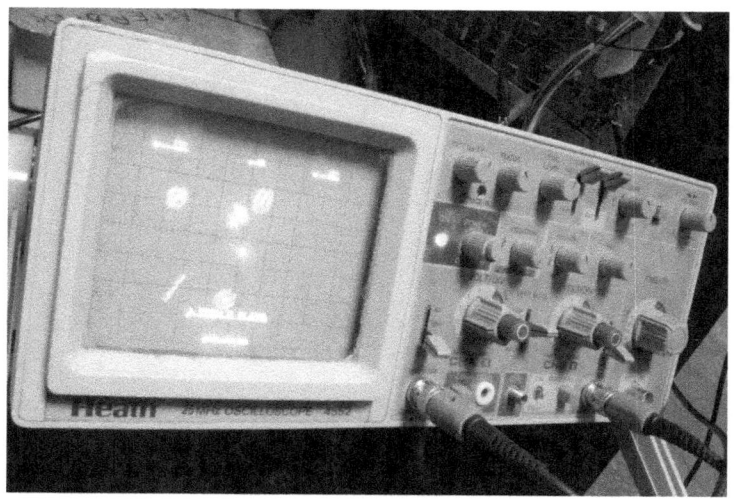

Wiring/Pinouts/Dipswitches

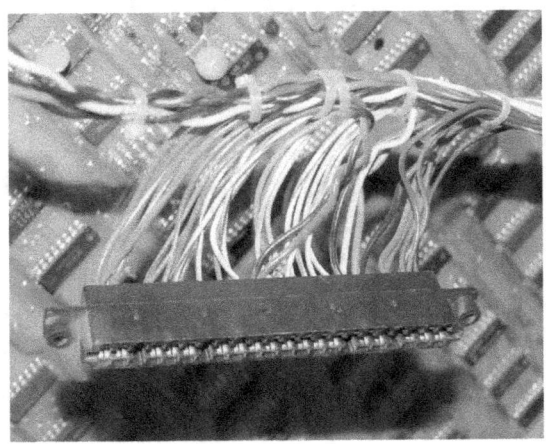

Game Board Main Connector Front (component side)

```
A GND
B +5V
C
D Counter Left
E Audio 2
F Counter Right
H
J Player 1
K Diagnostic Step
L Self Test
M Z Out
N Start 1
P Start 2
R Coin Right
S Rotate Left
T Fire
U X GND
V Y GND
W Reset
X 36 VAC
Y +5V
Z GND
```

Game Board Main Connector Back (solder side)

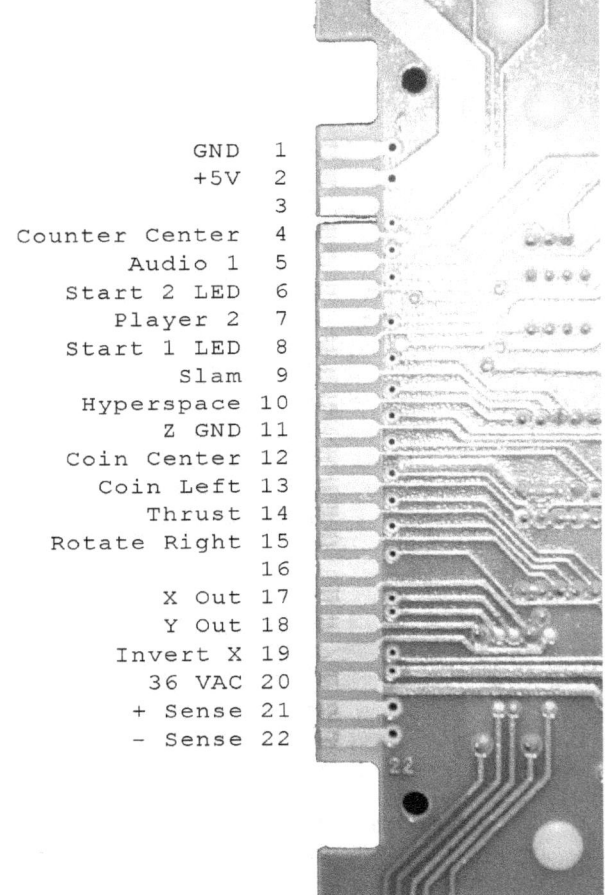

GND	1
+5V	2
	3
Counter Center	4
Audio 1	5
Start 2 LED	6
Player 2	7
Start 1 LED	8
Slam	9
Hyperspace	10
Z GND	11
Coin Center	12
Coin Left	13
Thrust	14
Rotate Right	15
	16
X Out	17
Y Out	18
Invert X	19
36 VAC	20
+ Sense	21
− Sense	22

Power Supply

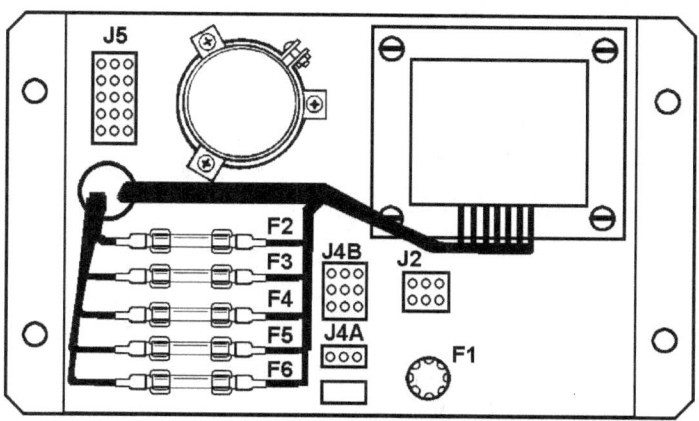

J1 Main AC In

1 - AC (Brown)
2 - Ground (Green/Yellow)
3 - AC Neutral (Blue)

J2 Power Switch & Interlocks

1 - AC (Brown)
2 - AC Neutral (Blue)
3 - not used
4 - To switches (Black)
5 - To switches (White)
6 - Ground (Green)

J3 / J4B Voltage Configuration Jumper

1 – 120V (Brown/Black)
2 – 100V (Red/Black)
3 – Common (Orange/Black)
4 – 120V (Black)
5 – 100V (Violet/Black)
6 – Common (White)

7 – 110V (White/Black)
8 – J2 Switches (Black)
9 – J2 Switches (White)

J4A Lighting

1 – AC (Black)
2 – Ground (Green)
3 – Common (White)

J5 Main Power Output

1 – 10.3V DC (Orange)
2 – 10.3V DC (Orange)
3 – 10.3V DC (Orange)
4 – Ground (Violet)
5 – Ground (Violet)
6 – 36V AC (Red)
7 – 36V AC (Red)
8 – 6.3V AC (Yellow)
9 – 6.3V AC (Yellow)
10 – 80V Isolated AC (Black)
11 – 65V AC (Brown)
12 – X-Y Return (Gray)
13 – 65V AC (Brown/White)
14 – 80V Isolated AC (Black)
15 - Ground

Regulator / Audio Board

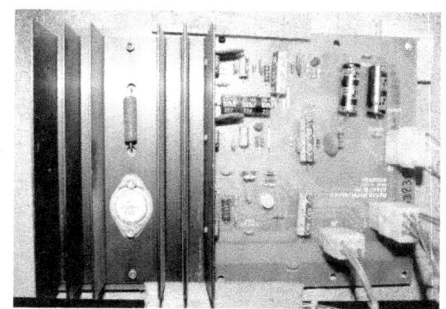

J6 Power Supply Input

1 - Ground
2 - Ground
3 – 10.6 V DC Unregulated
4 – Not Used
5 – Not Used
6 – 10.6 V DC Unregulated

J7 Regulated Output + Audio In

1 - +5V Return
2 – "-" Sense
3 – "+" Sense
4 - +5V Return
5 - +5V Regulated
6 - +5V Regulated
7 – Audio disable (not used)
8 – Audio Input 2
9 – Audio Input 1

J8 Speaker Audio Out

1 – Speaker 2 Return
2 – Speaker 1 Return
3 – Speaker 2
4 – Speaker 1

Coin Door

J55 Coin Door Plug

1 – Left Coin Switch Normally Open
2 – Center Coin Switch Normally Open
3 – Right Coin Switch Normally Open
4 – Test Switch
5 – Slam Switch
6 – Switch Ground
7 – 10V DC
8 – Left Coin Lockout Coil
9 – Center Coin Lockout Coil
10 – Right Coin Lockout Coil
11 – Not Used
12 – Not Used
13 – Right Coin Meter
14 – 10V DC
15 – Center Coin Meter
16 – 10V DC
17 – Left Coin Meter
18 – 10V DC
19 – 6.3V AC
20 – 6.3V AC Common
21 – Not Used
22 – Not Used
23 – Chassis Ground
24 – Chassis Ground

Game Adjustments via switches on Game Board

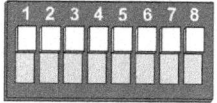

Dipswitch on top edge of board

1	2	3	4	5	6	7	8	
On	On							English
Off	On							German
On	Off							French
Off	Off							Spanish
		On						4 Ships
		Off						3 Ships
			On					Left Coin x 1
			Off					Left Coin x 2
				On	On			Right Coin x 1
				Off	On			Right Coin x 4
				On	Off			Right Coin x 5
				Off	Off			Right Coin x 6
						On	On	Free Play
						Off	On	1 Coin 2 Plays
						On	Off	1 Coin 1 Play
						Off	Off	2 Coins 1 Play

NOTES

_____

NOTES

NOTES

_____

NOTES

Other books by the same author